D1461449

You - As a Public Speaker

You - As a Public Speaker

DENNIS CASTLE

with a Foreword by
BASIL BOOTHROYD

Pelham Books

First published in Great Britain by PELHAM BOOKS LTD
52 Bedford Square, London WC1B 3EF
1974

ISBN 0 7207 0716 1

Set and printed in Great Britain by
Tonbridge Printers Ltd, Peach Hall Works, Tonbridge, Kent
in Baskerville eleven on twelve point on paper supplied by
P. F. Bingham Ltd, and bound by Dorstel Press,
Harlow

Dedicated to the Memory of
JACK HAWKINS C.B.E.
evergreen friend both in and
out of uniform who virtually
gave his life for the human
voice.

Kam ho chuka. Shukriya, colonel
sahib.

Contents

Acknowledgements

I raise my glass to propose a toast of thanks to. . . .

Basil Boothroyd, not only for his generous Foreword but for the pleasure of his company. I couple with his name the Savage Club which, it has been said, is entirely composed of actors, only the worst of whom were actually on the stage. Thus I remain indebted to its membership for some exhilarating conversation.

To the national and provincial press, radio and television, authors and publishers for their contributions to my education and being able to quote from some of them in these pages. To the Press Club itself which, for over twenty years of a much longer membership, has placed on me the onus of compèring its unique Fleet Street feasts of oratory and entertainment, granting me the rare privilege of meeting and hearing many of the world's great people.

To 'solo' helpers, Betty and Gordon Guy and David Niven, whom I have never met, but whose personal tribute to Jack Hawkins on television prompted my wording of the dedication. To Marie, my wife and friend, for her great patience and practical assistance on the typewriter; my publishers, Pelham, Alec Harrison – and a host of kind librarians who, down the years, have devoted so much time to my enquiries.

I recall, too, with equal gratitude, the encouragement of the late Ted Kavanagh, famous ITMA radio writer, who had such faith in me as a young speaker. And my long-gone parents who provided a home always bright with humour and enthusiasm. They are not part of my past – they will always belong to my present – even though I toast them now as 'Absent Friends'.

D.C.

Foreword by Basil Boothroyd

'One foot in Fleet Street, the other in the West End, but his elbows on the Savage Club bar.'

Ted Kavanagh was trying the impossible: to get Dennis Castle into a nutshell. It wasn't bad. But the Fleet Street bit means all kinds of writing, and the West End bit all kinds of acting: and you'd hardly put film studios, the Television Centre and Broadcasting House in the West End anyway. (Once on the radio Dennis was narrating Ibsen and doing a one-man comedy spot in the same week.)

He's a Lord's Taverner, a Water Rat, and a public speaker for all seasons. It was in a speech at one of the famous Press Club dinners, where he's introduced all the glittering names of our time for the past twenty years, that he referred to himself as a small-part player, a point taken up when the evening's guest of honour replied. 'If that speech was by a small-part player,' said Maurice Chevalier, 'what would we have got from a star?'

As to those elbows, it's certainly a membership hazard of the Savage Club to find Dennis Castle there. It isn't a club short on raconteurs, but he's the one most likely to make you miss your last train. Not that he latches on to you. You latch on to him. And then can't let go.

But telling jokes isn't making a speech, though, sadly, lots of people think so. They approach with a haggard look. 'I've got to make this speech. Do you know any stories?' They go off fortified with some terrible old lemon, make a hopeless mess of it, and wait for the laugh that didn't come before continuing, as scripted, 'But, seriously . . .' Agony all round.

All the same, if the humorous anecdote isn't the speech, it's a microcosm of it, in terms of construction, timing and delivery. The whole that encloses the part demands an equal respect for form, shape, lucidity, development and, perhaps most important, aptness to the occasion and context. If Dennis Castle can rock the Savage bar with stories about showbiz, which is one of his worlds, or cricket, which is another, and tell them in full dimension, painting the picture, citing the names and dates and places, controlling the suspense, impeccably judging the explosion point, it will also become clear from these pages that he knows all there is to know about the full-scale public utterance. Many don't, I fear, including plenty of our leading public utterers.

But you may, perhaps, when you've read how it's done. I say perhaps, not because I think the author will fail you. But you may fail the author. Don't think you can go right out and do it, that's all. Not just at first.

BASIL BOOTHROYD

Introduction

A psychologist's survey, published in 1974, and reported by Robert Chapman, to whom I am indebted, was compiled after questioning some 3,000 people on their most dreaded experience. There was the usual 'fears', 'flying in aircraft' (18 per cent) 'illness and death' (19 per cent), 'spiders and insects generally' (22 per cent), 'fright of heights' (32 per cent), together with many other understandable horrors, 'being buried alive', 'terror of the dark', and so on. But topping the list, at *forty-one per cent* in this research was *'fear of speaking in public'*!

Now obviously you are not among that group otherwise you would have shoved this book away unopened between 'Dracula' and 'Frankenstein' to avoid sleepless nights. But those figures do make tragic reading at a time when the world, more than ever in its history, needs a clear voice and the common sense of communication. Education is short of adequate staff, science is taking over the voice box, the click of ticker-tape seems to mean more than the human voice in a civilisation progressing only in gadgetry. Personality is slipping back; individualism is becoming the prerogative of the few.

The fear of addressing audiences goes way beyond just making a fool of ourselves in public. The real root of this lack of courage is inarticulacy. We know what we want to say but are not equipped with adequate vocabulary with which to express ourselves. We have no technique. The mind is jumbled, confused, in the search for the right dialogue to suit our purpose. Thus the extra tension of controlling ourselves before a sea of faces only adds to our feeling of insecurity. So, frustrated, we become bored. And bored people are always quarrelsome. It is not so much an inferiority complex as a lack of the right grounding – good conversation and exchange of ideas in the formative years.

In 1892 Herbert Asquith in a letter to Mrs Horner quoted the Theban in Herodotus . . . 'of all human troubles the most hateful is to feel that you have the capacity for power and yet have no field to exercise it'. There is a deep, foreboding loneliness in that statement. You feel you have a message but no medium in which to broadcast it. You think you have a purpose in life, but are confined within a cage. If you rip it apart, you are considered a vandal for destroying such a well-made cage.

Some speech-training instructors aver there is no such person as a born speaker. As a bald statement of fact it is true – but, while none of us entered the world with such an instinct, we could be lucky enough to have our beginnings in the right environment, a happy family atmosphere, good neighbours, enthusiastic teachers and extrovert school-mates who set us invigorating standards at an early age.

Such was my lot, my luck of the draw. I lived in a family, part musical, part theatrical, and was fortunate to be exposed to discussion, candour and laughter from birth. Certainly I was no born speaker – but, by example, at least I grew up *equipped* to be one.

Yet, as many of you may have found in similar surroundings, I found my family lovable but quite overpowering! The gift of the gab fomented in every aunt, uncle and cousin; my mother was a fine singer, my architect father was also a lecturer and my scenic artist grandfather a celebrated after-dinner speaker. They, none of them, had any fear of audiences. So good at it were they that, in the face of such competition, I grew up terrified of making a laughing stock of myself and blushed when having to utter my name aloud for the register on my first day at school.

Highly-strung, I edged my way through boarding school, avoiding any public appearance by a self-imposed withdrawal till I realised I was losing out. I found I either had to fight that hideaway instinct or all my developing ideas would remain dreams. So, like many, I gulped my way into amateur dramatics, losing my own tentative character by playing another. But it was the first positive step.

14

Although my parents sacrificed much to educate me, I left school possessing no achievement which qualified me automatically to earn a living – except a reasonable vocabulary. I became a solicitor's clerk. Quiet routine, I thought. But, to my horror, I found the law was not a retreat from public gaze after all. I had to face crowded courtrooms for my bread. Within my first fortnight I was appearing before county court registrars handling small debt cases. I died a thousand deaths at the prospect – but rose, quaking, and did it. And, later, *over*-did it! 'Young man,' came the admonishment from the Bench, 'do not dramatise this trivial case . . .' Indeed, my new-found confidence had turned me into a right 'ham'!

But even then, if some fortune-teller had revealed my true future, so daunting would the prospect have seemed, that I am certain I would have contemplated suicide. But who could believe that a pound-a-week clerk would one day become a professional actor facing critical theatre audiences, speak to millions on radio, have his face often on film and television screens, see his name on play bills, lecture officially in the Army in India, have some thirty thousand football fans fall silent to hear his public announcements at a first division ground (ever tried, when tense, to read 'East Fife four – Forfar five'?), chat away as compère to a packed Albert Hall, work with those belovedly-crazy Goons and speak in front of Royalty and Prime Ministers . . . ?

No, I would not have given credence to that crystal ball! Yet – it happened. It has been my life.

I cite these scenes not as a boast but still half-stupified that such was my destiny. It does not represent talent so much as a conquest of fear. I have always been keenly aware of my limitations and know I lack star quality. But I feel secure on the lower rungs of my several ladders simply because I never expected even to set foot on them in the first place!

I have survived, not entirely unscarred of course but, in my minor way, I have got out of life far more than I ever expected. I have raised laughter, been listened to seriously on discussion panels, made a thousand speeches and heard applause meant for me. That I can, after all these years, still surprise myself, makes all other disappointments worthwhile.

All I have picked up I learned by trial and error. Not as

some pundits would have approved, perhaps, but there is no learning better than having to rectify your own mistakes unaided. And if you care to name any mistakes in the public appearance business, I have made them. Gaffes galore! Once owing to being wrongly briefed by the organisers, I had to apologise in public . . . and when you've done that, you've done everything!

So, with confidence growing over the years, I've been able to cope with most public speaking hazards without panic. That is why I hope this book will help you set out on the essential road of communication and overcome any doubts you may have in your own ability to face audiences. You can astonish yourself, as I did. And there is no inner joy more complete than achieving an ambition we once considered within our secret selves to be a fantasy utterly beyond our reach. Then . . . 'My God, they're applauding me – I've done it!' That exultation when you find you have not only got your message across but succeeded beyond your wildest dreams is the greatest education of all.

It means, in short, you are able to communicate. And that makes you a very useful citizen indeed.

D.C.

CHAPTER ONE

The Way Ahead

From the moment we utter our first cry as the midwife smacks our bottom, we begin a life of personal appearances. As soon as we gurgle 'mumma' or 'dadda' according to which Freudian slip we make first, we are destined to be many times in the limelight. We may not seek it, be shy and cowering, but there will be moments in our earthly time when all eyes are on us, the solitary, pin-pointed individual who has to speak alone across a crowded room.

To some, brought up in an extrovert environment, public speaking and dominating a sea of faces confidently will become second-nature. Others the public eye will quell and any spotlight remain an ulcerous nightmare for life, an obstacle to their social or working happiness never to be overcome. But, to us, the middle-line majority, it may begin as a strain, an anxiety, which we can defeat by disciplined practice eventually to enjoy appearing in public.

The variations of our metabolism belong to the psychiatrist's couch rather than these pages. Sufficient for our purpose therefore is the fact that our nervous system and adrenalin workings differ considerably from our neighbour's and one cannot expect exactly the same result from two people whose inheritances are of different genes and backgrounds. Temperament, both inborn and developed by environment, lies within the mysteries of that haunted house we call a brain and we have to live with whichever hot or cold nerve system fate designed especially for us.

Once the more retiring citizens could find a niche for themselves, working quietly in the background, and still be successful. Rarely, if ever, would they be called upon to speak in public. They put their brain power on paper for others to talk about. But today few men or women can be at the top in their work unless they have the ability to stand up and speak. No longer can firms afford to retain the inarticulate chairman, seated there by inheritance or some roster system. Key people in control now require to face audiences. You not only have to hold your job down to your own satisfaction, but be seen to be doing it well by those in your charge. If you are hesitant or limited in vocabulary, you may well not do justice to the most brilliant schemes you present. Should you be too inarticulate to explain your expertise lucidly and with authority, those around you will question your ability. So if you are not to be in a back-room all your life, you need to speak well in public.

Not only does this apply to industry and commerce but also in our art and social worlds. Many restricted to chanting slogans in a crowd cannot defend themselves individually. When asked to state their specific case, an audience terrifies them. Thus they become easy victims of compromising propaganda. Some try to mask ignorance with insolence and so, sadly, often pay higher penalties for failure than others who have the confidence to speak up without stage-fright. And too often authority regards the silence of incomprehension as dumb mutiny and deals with it as such. It is not progress and makes for much medieval justice.

Personal appearances take many forms. However much you may shun the limelight, it will be constantly picking you out to say a few words. Not necessarily in a speech to a relaxed audience but in a witness box or before a committee or appointments board when your very future may depend on you showing a bold front. There might be a turning point in conversation or discussion in an office, bar or living-room where you can supply the vitally apposite remark or suggestion which impresses influential hearers to your advantage. But all too often we remain silent and only rehearse what we might have said in the car or train going home, far too late to be of any use to us — even though we may well tell our friends we did say it! We would like to have spoken our minds, but perhaps we lacked sufficient guts – or possibly vocabulary – to contribute and so perhaps, allowed a more erudite person to win the day on a completely false argument.

People hooked by television and radio no longer attempt to find out about each other. The mechanical box supplies all their needs – or so they think. They do not consider their neighbours can be in the least interesting and they will not bother to turn off the 'telly' if there is an unexpected caller. Conversation and exchange of ideas is perhaps at its lowest ebb this century. The apathetic attitude of being entertained rather than providing it for ourselves leads to far too much second-hand thinking and the parroting of clichés. Personality becomes eroded through lack of use and self-imposed ignorance. Some stopped learning when they left school – even if they learned much there anyway. They cannot be blamed for their lack of adult application – they were obviously given a poor start in life.

Of course conscientious self-taught folk without happy family backgrounds are often more sincere and convincing than the privileged academics simply because they have suffered the experience of hardship far more than those whose feet were firmly guided on the right path in childhood. But both, in order to be able to impart their knowledge, have the initial hurdle of facing audiences. And only by the courage of their convictions can they succeed. It is not everyone's cup of tea, as witness that forty-one per cent I mentioned in my Introduction. But more of us must achieve it if world communication is to survive . . . someone must pass on the increasing technology, arts and crafts – and blend it with compassion and good humour.

The fact that you are reading this book shows you want to try. That is half the battle won already.

Who Are You?

No one can put a mirror to his mind. Yet before you can speak responsibly in public you must dissect your own character, for speech-making can be a dangerous opportunity to act as we *think* we should rather than as nature made us. We are liable to see ourselves as heroes, shrewd cookies or svelt intellectuals when, in reality, we fall far short of such imaginative self-portraits.

We put on a charade as someone else to cover nerves or a feeling of inadequacy. Television impersonator Mike Yarwood, in an interview, confessed that his gift of mimicry was used, even as a child, to hide his innate shyness. This frank admission from such a brilliant professional entertainer applies equally to us in our smaller world of public appearance. But while he has been able to turn his gift to advantage, 'doing to the life' famous people, we have only ourselves to impersonate – and will do that amateurishly if we are foolish enough to try.

We cannot see ourselves as others see us, however much we think we can. We cannot win by altering our inborn style. One can change habits by will-power, opinions by experience and outward appearance by choice, but our personality remains constant, peculiar to us and unchangeable. Only a consummate actor can falsify his personality and then only for short periods speaking special lines written for the role. But if he has to invent those lines for himself he would revert to his own true character to speak them. Our inherited personality remains and we are unwise if we pretend that we are greater or smaller than nature made us.

Thus, when you embark upon the choppy seas of public speaking you must know yourself; truly know yourself, ruthlessly and fearlessly. It is not easy: but audiences are very perceptive. The man who thinks he appears before them as generous, affable and self-effacing may well give the impression of self-satisfaction, an unctious do-gooder, patronising and mock-modest. The woman who feels she exudes good cheer, neighbourly love and practical advice could be considered by those hearing her as a 'know-all', completely obsessed with other people's affairs. It is the 'assumed' role in a speaker which embarrasses listeners . . . the thoroughly model husband who pretends, by arch implication, that he is a great womanizer, the small businessman who swells into a philosophising tycoon or the insignificant social climber who name-drops . . . they all get levelled out in front of shrewd audiences.

Often such attitudes are forgivable as they are a form of pride and stout defiance against the rigours of daily life, a reassurance that you *are* somebody – but you still cannot escape yourself. Most of us are pessimists about others' chances and optimistic about our own. It is a form of superstition, 'lucky-white-heather' thinking. It is human to try and be as good – or better – than the next man, but can we always honestly supply tangible proof beyond pipe-dreams? Walter Mittyism is understandable in a grey, fierce, greedy world but, if it shows through in public speaking, you risk derision rather than earn praise.

So, when you enter the public speaking ranks in any form, give yourself a detailed check-up first. Analyse every facet of your true colours without prejudice. Weaknesses are hard to admit but, to succeed, all intolerances and Achilles heels must be taken into account. Including short tempers! It is a tough assignment but, in the long term, you will find that you will enjoy facing audiences as yourself rather than put on an act. And, believe me, it makes the job far easier!

Sincerity

...which is the keynote to all good speaking of course. Bernard Levin once used the phrase 'the ritual of constant pretence' which, in his opinion, too many M.P.s used in the House of Commons. This aptly describes some speakers in all other fields of public speaking. We have all heard it, a hypo-critical approach, a synthetic charm oozing insincerity, some high-minded 'reasons' covering, in reality, pretty devious moti-vations. It goes on from the shop-floor to the board-room.

Sincerity is not always candour. We would be very lonely citizens indeed if we practised complete sincerity throughout our lives. The whole truth and nothing but the truth is necessary only when reputation or justice is at stake. But to volunteer the truth unasked can be mere spite. Uninhibited sincerity can hurt feelings quite unnecessarily. When someone asks what you think of her new hat, you don't tell her she looks terrible in it. You accede to her need of reassurance simply because it is relatively unimportant. She bought the hat, it was her choice, so let her enjoy it. The white lie can, in itself, be a form of sincerity, a diplomatic, human tactic to avoid offence or dis-illusionment.

This applies to public speaking. The art, in its broadest form, is the knack of persuasion without hoodwinking. One may gild the lily if it is not being patently dishonest. In commer-cial speaking sincerity should be a paramount ingredient but, even in a light-hearted speech, you still have to persuade the audience to enjoy itself. And you can only succeed if you believe sincerely that what you are saying is of true value to them either as instruction or entertainment.

Vanity

Of course you must possess a certain diluted vanity to speak publicly. Unless through civic or business position obliging us to face audiences consistently, many of us would not try to do it at all. But we do. We think we have something to offer, even find the applause at the end an opiate, and, perhaps making us better citizens to live with! But we must make our speaking ambitions acceptable not only to ourselves but to our listeners. We must not expect audiences to take our offerings entirely without question. We may think we are God's gift to the speaking world – but it is not what we think of ourselves which counts in the end.

When asked to speak in public what is the first thought which crosses your mind? My certain bet is that you will think as I did – *'How can I impress 'em?'* Human, understandable – but only valid to a lesser extent . . . for that approach lacks that vital ingredient of sincerity. We are vain enough to consider ourselves more important than our subject. To be successful the initial reaction should be : *'How can I treat my subject to please the audience?'* And if you tackle the job in that frame of mind and so please the audience – then you *will* impress them. You can't miss! But if we set out to show *ourselves* off we can fall flat on our red, embarrassed faces.

That then is your first brief. Substitute 'What can the subject do for me?' by 'What can I do for the subject' and always work on that principle.

Admittedly a speech *is* a form of self-portrait. When you rise to speak you at once present the audience with a picture of yourself. At that brief but critical moment your subject is not in their minds at all – they react to the sight of you. So, if you have some exaggerated vision of yourself, the picture you project may well be a cartoon, transparency or blatant commercial!

You have only to think back to your early schooldays. When new teachers entered the classroom for the first time their qualifications did not interest you, just how they looked – and sounded. It was only later that you equated their personalities with their subjects. And, as you will remember, some seemed ideal while others were odd-ball misfits. So it is with public speaking. You must develop according to your true endowments, not in some trumped-up image of yourself.

It is not vanity, however, to wish to be popular. Obviously you must aim to please audiences. No one will listen to you rationally if they hate your guts. But you must be liked for yourself. Once you appear 'clever', audiences will shy away from you. You have to strike the middle road between undue modesty and self-satisfaction. And you can only do this by knowing your subject so intimately that it becomes part of your character and needs no contrived tricks to present it.

Style

Bernard Shaw said; 'He who has nothing to assert has no style and can have none. He who has something to assert will go far in the power of style . . . his convictions will carry him . . .'

A good speaker with style does not consciously show others how to do the job – but nevertheless stands out as a fine example. Style cannot be cultivated save by experience in facing audiences sincerely. Style is not a conceit, a wilfully commanding presence, but a natural charm, an unaffected aura of confidence, repose and reliability. Few can wittingly possess it for it requires that you are completely devoid of any falsity . . . but style can be acquired if you are truly sure of your subjects.

Style is not a question of sartorial appearance either, although a good dress sense helps. But a speaker with style has a natural presence and, as he or she begins to talk, the audience settles back almost as one man, with a reaction of relaxed pleasure knowing the speaker has flair and the job is in expert hands.

Types of Speeches

Speech-making falls into two distinct categories, the personal and the technical. Under these two main headings there are of course many variations but, for the moment, we will just concern ourselves with the difference between them.

The *personal* speech is one you construct entirely from your own material, adapted to meet the requirements of a general brief on a social occasion. It may be proposing or replying to a toast, a wedding speech, a welcome to some V.I.P. or a prize presentation. You know the framework, but colour the canvas within it by your own ingenuity.

The *technical* speech is an already-designed canvas which you frame as attractively as possible. The ingredients, the data, surveys, figures, and so on, are already prepared. You cannot leave out any facts, but you do your best to humanise them so that your audience does not nod off during your discourse. But whether an advertising campaign, shareholders' meeting or annual report, you have to strike the tricky medium of not swamping the facts with your personality nor yet again let them kill you stone dead as a character.

Most of us, however, start in the social sphere. Usually a club or society wants someone to propose a toast at a dinner. These are conventional requests but that does not mean that your speech must be hidebound by local tradition. Certainly your material must include relevant points but do not, as many do in early days of public speaking, stand up and more or less copy last year's speaker. Be yourself, adjust the ritual if you like so that it at least sounds original in your hands. Too often new speakers are content to follow the plough of time-worn clichés .... 'It gives me very great pleasure ...' (when the strained look on his face indicates the reverse) ... 'I am much honoured ...' (when a committee have shanghaied him to speak because they cannot find anyone else) ... 'the pleasant task before me ...' (delivered as if with a smell under his nose) ... and so on, every phrase from the local mayor's book.

Now, where I have put those brackets above can indicate an entirely different approach. Depending where you are, of course, you can treat the subject quite entertainingly by revealing something of the backstage arrangements ... 'I am sure our honoured guest will understand me when I say this speech does not give me very great pleasure ... I'm frightened out of my life. Press-ganged by the committee ...' and so on, a good natured leg-pull. If you are already known to the audience such an approach can be highly diverting, always provided you do not insult anyone by over-playing it!

Then again, your first speaking brief might be on a more serious occasion. At your school, university or firm there is more onus on you to make an impact – and sometimes less scope within which to do it. Indeed, with a firm, your career might be in the balance – a good speech could earmark you for promotion, a bad one retard your progress. So it is essential that you play safe, not put on any act or be ultra-adventurous. You stick rigidly to your subject but phrase it interestingly so that those listening can see that a lot of original thought has gone into it.

The Need For a Good Working Vocabulary
The beautiful dolly bird is stopped in the street by a television interviewer. In front of camera he asks her : 'Do you feel beauty contests are a form of slave market?'

She smiles gloriously – then – tragedy – she begins to speak.

'Dun know whatyer mean? . . . Well . . . I mean . . . er . . . they're nice, ent they? Booty contests, I mean . . . I like 'em . . . yer know what I mean? They're good, ent they? I mean . . . there's prizes . . . an' things . . . yew git on the telly, tew, don't yer . . . . fab clothes . . . git free make-up . . . lots uv bread if yer win . . . which is nice, innit . . . if yer know what I mean. . .'

So the pretty kid stumbles on, obviously groping all the time for inspiration, searching for alternative words to describe her mazed thoughts – but the requisite vocabulary is not in her brain in the first place. The result is an embarrassing, incoherent shambles and a waste of the viewers' time. Not the girl's fault but God help her marriage when the bed loses interest. And her children? What will they ever learn from her inarticulate ramblings?

To speak well both in public and in ordinary conversation you need a good working vocabulary. Not a selection of sophisticated, high-flown phrases or gimmicks you file away just for speeches, but ordinary, everyday words which can be understood by everyone and yet contain sufficient variety to enhance your information to make it more compelling.

Take time out with a dictionary and also become more analytical in your reading. Have deeper conversations with others, join debating societies, acting groups and both chat and listen. Do not remain content with monosyllabic necessities just to make yourself heard above juke boxes or discotheques – they have their place but not in the vicinity of good conversation or exchange of ideas. Noise pollution is not only deafening us but also slaying communication generally.

Perhaps background cacophony is one reason why too many young people in this so-called enlightened age, are restricted in vocabulary to bare synonyms and antonyms of life, 'Yes/No', 'Good/Bad', 'Nice/Nasty', 'Love/Hate'. They have no further degrees of meaning or finesse in their vocabulary and this drastically reduces the status of individuals so unluckily limited. Chances of attainment will be few if they lack word power.

Grammar

Some are apt to think of grammar as being unnecessary so long as they are even vaguely understood. In fact good grammar is often considered a form of class distinction! Yet if only those who ignore it through sheer lazy-mindedness could be made to understand what they are losing they would realise the terrible disadvantage they suffer. If all other qualifications are equal, a job will go to the better spoken of two applicants. That is not prejudice but absolute common sense: the telephone and letter dictation is vital in the business world.

One can aimlessly kick a football in the street but it takes the grammar of the game, the control, the artistry and virtuosity to make a first-class player. You can pile brick upon brick and make some sort of temporary shelter but, if you want to build a house, the precise grammar of architecture is required. The television experts must know the grammar of set design, lighting, script and voice projection. A sound knowledge of grammar is merely equipping oneself to make a decent job of communicating with others. Considering the progress made in other directions, speech is very backward in Britain. And if speech falls short, somebody one day will misunderstand and press the wrong knob.

Some are opposed, violently opposed, to good speaking, usually as a façade to cover inadequacy. Yet more than ever we find ourselves conversing with overseas business people. Only if we speak intelligently will we make our English understood.

Equip yourself with a good thesaurus — Roget's is a most popular one — which gives you a complete coverage on word variation. Unlike the dictionary which gives you single word meanings, a thesaurus is designed to help you find the most appropriate word to suit any situation or idea. For example, the simple word 'wish', has many connotations. 'Ambition', 'fancy', 'inclination', 'partiality', 'a penchant for', 'aspiration', 'desire' and many more. These, as you have seen, are not just alternative words for 'wish'. They represent other aspects or forms of 'wishing'. You would not say you were 'partial to becoming a good speaker', but you could say 'you wish to be', that 'you desire to be', 'aspire to be' or even have 'ambitions to be a good speaker'. Each has subtle differences.

That is what is meant by a good working vocabulary; knowing which shade of sense to use in certain contexts to make your words more personal and colourful. But, if through a sadly deprived upbringing you are stuck for life with 'wish' and an existence of similar monosyllables, you are not going to get far in conversation, let alone on a public platform. Such handicapped people have to leave others to solve their problems – so they can be manipulated or advantage taken of them.

Language is a beautiful, vital accomplishment, enabling us to express ourselves beyond the mundane. Shelley said: 'Speech creates thought.' We can give a radiance both to our subjects and our personalities with well-chosen phrases; we can avoid disaster by using the right word in the right place and add humour and romance to lives drabber than our own. Words are a necessity even beyond sight and even the tragically deaf can at least read fine words. But to be dumb – to see but be unable to express oneself, to be deprived of saying 'I love you', to hear perhaps but be unable to answer, is a hell hard to imagine.

Study again my dedication in the front of this book, those who feign to despise vocabulary and would mis-use their voices and the heritage of their language. And kids who want to be film stars? How can they be instructed that such people as Jack Hawkins reached the top because they could speak clearly and understood words?

Obviously you will already be well equipped with normal word power to be reading this book, but it does no harm to check a grammar book every now and again. Nerves will not play nearly as big a part when you stand up to speak if you are certain of both vocabulary and construction.

Word Distinctions and Misapplications
Misuse of words often happens through over-cursory reading and skipping of newspapers. You half digest a word but think

you have it pat. And so you use it without checking first. Hence, in normal conversation, some people do not distinguish between 'effect' and 'affect'. 'Cold weather doesn't effect me,' says one, while another says : 'the pills had no affect on me . . .'

You may say 'disinterested' when you mean 'uninterested', a common mistake. 'Disinterested' means 'unbiased' like a tennis umpire for example. He participates in the game interpreting its laws but is 'disinterested' in who wins. But if he was 'uninterested' he would dislike tennis and would not be perched up on that ladder. Yet we so often hear 'disinterested' to denote complete disassociation, the 'couldn't care less' attitude.

You can distinguish between the *'un'* and *'dis'* words another way. 'Disgraceful' means something offensive while 'ungraceful' means coltish or shambling, like a capering dancer lacking co-ordination. 'Disarrayed' means untidy, but 'unarrayed' can mean not clothed.

At the party a guest says; 'D'you mind, I've *bought* my girl friend' as if he's just paid for her at the supermarket. 'Brought' and 'bought' are often confused. Some still use 'learn' for 'teach' . . . but one must remember that a pupil learns, the tutor teaches. One could fill a whole book with these misapplications so these examples are merely to put you on your guard.

I know several qualified men and women who speak badly and cannot even spell tolerably well. They always justify their self-imposed handicap with the languid answer that so long as they are understood, what else matters? Frankly it does – a great deal. Laziness in vocabulary leads to other slothful behaviour. We must be able to converse with each other in an interesting way beyond mere cavemen grunts. These extremists who despise clarity of diction and word strength are in mortal danger of returning to ancient British primitivism through lack of intelligent communication.

Words do get mauled around as generations change them, usually by increasing their meaning. So a study of them will not come amiss when you begin serious public speaking. One can only give limited guidelines in a book like this but if you decide to use an unfamiliar word which you feel suits your purpose, check it in the dictionary. It will also give you a phonetic pronunciation to help you as well.

The Jargon Johnnies

We live in a world of commercial catch-phrases too . . . 'escalate', 'middle-mass', 'senior salariat', 'price-wise', 'client-wise' – and much of it a complete waste, 'time-wise'. 'Gimmick' is an ugly but 'meaningful' word. But the jargon johnnies purposely seek gimmicky words with which to sound important, a sort of 'ad-man's' esperanto. They are also 'parenthesis' boys, who live in a world of 'top brackets', 'study brackets', 'income brackets' – and one day they will coin 'racket brackets', mark my words! It will become part of their 'norm' . . .

Most of this is ponderously stupid and certainly bewilders the man in the street just at a time when he needs absolute clarification of his problems. So, please, when you are speaking in public, do not fall into the jargon trap too easily. Some would blind us with a sort of quasi-scientific vocabulary and anger the less educated (and therefore the more militant) who see it as smoke screens hiding some guile against them. And very often they are, like the small print in some hire-purchase contracts.

It is all too easy for verbiage voyeurs to muck around with words in their 'think tank'. And always the result is ugly, contrived and pretentious, not really good for their 'charisma'! W. H. Auden summed it up on television once when he said: 'When you blow a thing to bits now you call it "disassembly".'

I have often heard a good speech ruined by the introduction of one outlandish word. The speaker has obviously 'worked it in', obsessed with using it, come hell or high water. His speech has been uncomplicated and interesting until he suddenly utters: 'Floccinaucinihilipilification'. Wham! You stop thinking about the rest of the speech at once. How the blazes are we to know that that extraordinary latin-rooted word means 'estimating as worthless' – or that it is – or was – one of the longest words in existence? So we end up merely in estimating that speaker as worthless.

I use these crazy examples to emphasise the need of a balanced vocabulary for your audiences. Going over their heads is a shocking vanity. Of course there are always grammar pundits who deplore any deviation from syntax but, with commonsense, a vocabulary must move with the times. What most rational audiences object to is change for the sake of change, or being unprogressively 'trendy', if you like. In a generation or two the long term 'effect' may 'affect' our computers. They won't understand what we are saying, bless their programmed innards and give us our 'come-uppance' by disassembling us!

Economy of words means that, when you have been allotted ten minutes to make your speech, you do not waste valuable time by useless padding. My favourite quotation from Shakespeare is one of the finest examples of sheer beauty of economy. Hamlet's mother, Gertrude, in describing Ophelia's drowning, begins with a simple but to me beautiful line: 'There is a willow grows aslant a brook . . .'

Just study those eight words again. Note the rhythm and symmetry of the phrase – and its complete simplicity. Now try if you can to use a substitute for 'aslant'. 'Leaning', 'bending', 'slanting', 'angled'? But none can better Shakespeare's 'aslant'. It is poetic, I agree, but I am using it as an example of how simple brevity can sound pleasant to the ear. If you can write speeches with one vital word per sentence that lifts it beyond the ordinary, then you will go far.

The Art of Listening and Conversation

A young girl once said to me: 'I think the world has stopped listening' and bless her student scarf, she is darned near right!

Too many of us are inclined to talk too much, preferring to repeat our own stale anecdotes or opinions rather than listen to others. It boils down to preferring to hold the floor ourselves than give others the chance. Sheer vanity of course – but also stupid. If we do not listen we cannot learn. No sincere speaker should be guilty of permanent limelight – desire in ordinary conversation. Give ear to those around you; they can stimulate your mind with new arguments and angles, new stories – even new words.

Listen to radio. It is better than television because you have also to exercise your mind by forming your own imagined picture to match the dialogue. Television does not allow you to play more than a passive role, although study of speakers in the medium is always useful. Keep a writing pad by your set and make a note of any word you think might be valuable to you.

Get out and about and widen your social scene all you can. Some see only the same people, day after day, at work or in the home and rarely meet a stranger. If they do, the result is that they treat them with suspicion and a sort of 'on guard' intolerance. So they remain completely in a one-track world, useless to their conversation, let alone public speaking.

The seeds of good public speaking are sown from good conversation.

Repetition

Politicians indulge in it a great deal to plant home points. 'We are the party to bring down inflation, we are the party to increase wages, we are the party to improve housing . . .' They may use that repetition as much as ten times in the same speech. The Americans are past masters at it; it has become a Presidential trend over the years just as speaking in mock-Churchillian tones is still the 'in-thing' with some of our members of parliament.

But avoid repetition in a speech when you can. It wastes time unless you are talking scholastically or instructing young students. In a social speech it smacks of dogma. Long-winded repetition is a politican's prerogative – they love ditto repeato tactics – but then perhaps they are also trying to convince themselves . . .

Use of Slang and Colloquialisms

The purists hate any divergence from the straight and narrow of the grammar book but, if some 'way-out' term suits some breezy occasion, then use it. Not all the time, of course, but where applicable, in anecdote or to contrast or highlight some specific point. Provided the word is generally accepted and understood and has a genuine place in the speech, don't be afraid to include it.

Terming oneself a 'square' is, for example one of the most popular slang terms which indicates older groups in relation to modern youth. Speech-makers use it constantly but it has had such a vogue among the more mature citizens that I gather the young inventors have now outlawed it from their own dialogue. Perhaps they resented even our acceptance of it. However, sadly, older folks do seem to have a broader sense of humour than the young so they go on using 'square' against themselves – and a very apt term it is.

But where so-called 'trendy' terms do sound wrong in public speaking is when you try to reproduce such ordinary conversation as a speech. I once heard a young lass deliver a talk entirely in 'kaff' (café) dialogue. She tried to sound 'mod, perhaps in defiance of the middle-aged majority in her audience, but frankly she gave the impression she was not so much 'with-it' as without it. She was talking about contemporary drama but used 'I couldn't care less', 'you can say that again' (when we had said nothing!) 'not on your nelly', 'get knotted' and 'drop dead', (an offensive and disturbing term to any audience). She also constantly used that absurd, breath-wasting qualification . . . 'I had to put my make-up on, didn't I?' (it should have been 'hadn't I' anyway) till we in the audience lost all thread of her talk – didn't we!

This ending of a sentence with a request for understanding is part of the tetchiness of our times. Actually it is a pointless mannerism beloved of television script-writers who erroneously put it into the mouths of Victorian and Edwardian characters, feeling obliged to force it in every programme. Many of these terms are also beloved of disc jockeys and so are taken as guide lines by the more impressionable but less intelligent of their listeners.

However I am not knocking youth. There will always be copyists in every generation, slaves to the catch-phrase. All age groups have their idiosyncracies. We all know some woman who affixes, 'yes, well,' to every sentence she utters. Or repeats . . . 'I said to her, I said, Mrs Jones, I said,' Some of these make public speeches too! But it is a trait that must be conquered by concentration. My advice is only use one salient catch phrase or slang term per speech. Then it will have far more impact.

Knowing Your Limitations

When you begin public speaking it is pardonable to feel capable of perfection. It is the right attitude, but temper it with logic. Unless brushed with genius (and who will recognise it?) ninety-nine per cent of us are average people with only odd gifts in certain directions. We can only reach our particular stratum of success by hard graft and experience, by trial and error and knowing just how far we can go before over-reaching ourselves. Knowing our own limitations is vital to speech-making.

You see, by standing up in public to speak you are also tackling the most difficult job in showbusiness – that of a solo performer. You have no supporting players to get you out of trouble if you fluff your lines and, if you make a mistake, there can be no television or film 're-takes' to get your scene right. No, you are faced with a 'live' audience out there – all eyes on you alone, entirely the master or mistress of your own fate – and only yourself to blame if you fail. But then to succeed is all the sweeter for indeed it can be attributed entirely to your own work.

That is why, at the onset of a speaking career, you must consider carefully all your qualifications and capabilities. These will increase, of course, speech by speech, as you do the rounds in varying forms of public appearance. You will, no doubt, adopt little artifices peculiar to yourself to increase your presentation of subjects, but provided they are aimed at delighting the audience rather than self-conceit, you will be accepted as an accomplished speaker.

Speaking is an art with wide connotations. It has rules and formats which have to be followed by widely diverse speakers, none of whom are exactly alike. Obviously there are limits to what each man or woman can do with the millions of subjects likely to be selected for speeches. Some will be better equipped in one field than another, while others may be more versatile. So you have to sort yourself out, not only in your subjects but in presentation and style. If you tend to prefer humour then highly-emotive or academic speeches are not for you – yet. But you may well develop an ability in these directions as you gain experience, repose and knowledge.

However, to begin with we must first taste that cold porridge of self-analysis and see what attributes we already possess to our advantage at the onset. How do we study our true form to make the best of it?

Horses for Courses

That old racing adage is one we can well apply to ourselves. Some horses prefer hard going, others soft, some sprint only the short distances, others have stamina for the long race. Some are temperamental, coltish or docile. Others rear up in fright at the starting-gate, while some trot in quite unaffected. Some prefer the 'flat', others go well over fences. And we need that sort of horse-sense about ourselves. Which course suits us best in the Speaking Stakes? How can we start well up in the betting rather than as long-shot outsiders?

In early speaking engagements there are bound to be a few bumpy rides while you are in the apprentice stage but, from that garnering of experience, you will find which occasions afford you, personally, most scope and those which really are not yet your track. Then, as the years pass, you will be able to tackle more and more subjects and functions simply because you can then not only adjust your personality to suit them – but also your word power.

But do not confuse a realisation of talent boundaries with an inferiority complex. A gold-medal athlete or champion boxer is probably a poor after-dinner speaker – good at his job but weak at explaining it. It is common sense to know the extent of your range, especially early on, for it saves the miseries of getting out of your depth in front of unsympathetic audiences. We will know that we can be light-hearted, serious, witty or philosophical according to our natures. We know what subjects we can tackle convincingly and those for which our knowledge is too superficial to attempt at the moment. We will know our vocabulary and our voice range – of which more anon – and so not miscaste ourselves in unsuitable roles at the onset. Then gradually, almost imperceptibly, our compass will widen to more extended points.

Showmanship and Entertainment

Keeping within one's limitations also does not mean that we must face the public entirely devoid of showmanship. That is an accepted and necessary facet under any conditions of public speaking from the pulpit to the bedside manner.

My train has run an hour late and I leave it fuming and foul-tempered. Then high up in the station roof a lady announcer's voice apologises for the delay. She sounds personally distressed that I have been so inconvenienced. Immediately I look at the amplifier and think . . . 'It's not your fault, my dear . . .' and am placated. The railway are using 'showman-

34

ship'. A man's voice would only further irritate travellers – but a lady is the right filly for that tricky course.

Showmanship, contrary to most conceptions, is not spectacular effect but a calculated technique designed to get the most out of your particular prowess. Certainly showmanship is not insincere. It enhances your speech, infuses originality and panache into the presentation of your subject. Many staid, ritualistic 'toasts' and 'formal banquet' speeches certainly need the blood transfusion of showmanship to lift them above mediocrity. You do not have to lose sight of your subject to give it novelty of approach. Rather you should tackle a speech with a feeling of carte blanche, a servant to the subject but not servile to it.

A speech, however academic or technical, must also be entertaining to get through to the listeners. You have only to think back to your schooldays. Few of us could react with enthusiasm to the number of apples we could purchase for so many pence or tackle eagerly the useless problem of how long it took a bath full of holes to empty itself. But if those mathematics had been equated to football league tables, cricket averages or buying pop star discs at so much each per month – then most children would have found the topicality entertaining – and so absorb the instruction.

Some die-hards hate the word 'entertainment' in relation to speeches. They associate it with jokes and laughter, at which most formal elocutionists are poor exponents anyway, preferring as they do to 'impress' rather than 'amuse'. To some pundits causing 'levity' is a low form of speaking! But they are not the judges – the audiences are! And even a funeral oration needs a certain dignified showmanship to make it effective. An ebullient speaker can hold his audiences agog, or a quiet, less demonstrative type keep them enthralled simply by using showmanship and being entertaining within their subject.

When speaking in public, it is easy to bore; the real task is to entertain.

Confidence and Nervousness

We feel we have something to offer in the public speaking world, perhaps impress people with our wit or argument. But, like singing in the bath, we would not suddenly like to find ourselves on stage at Covent Garden. So just how confident are we?

We may see ourselves, in our mind's image, as challenging and in control as the Prime Minister in the House, ready with rapier wit to put the Opposition in place but, when our moment comes and we rise to speak, we find our mouth dry and not only butterflies in the stomach but a swarm of bees as well! So how much will nerves reduce our impact? For they do, you know, early on in speaking dates. We might be brave enough before a mirror alone at home – but when you see all those faces upturned towards you and hear the announcement of your name . . . 'pray silence for . . .' that is when *you* pray! All that original rehearsal courage seems to ebb away and we rise halting and uncertain, our minds a momentary blank.

That loneliness happens to everyone first time out – and even in subsequent speeches until experience makes them first-nature. But if you did not have nerves you would probably never make a good speech. Nerves are a compliment to the audience. You want to please them, are anxious not to let them down. So you become tense in anticipation of the ordeal ahead. Perhaps, too, other speakers before you on that occasion have made it look all too easy by their expertise. Suddenly you feel personally inadequate.

I find that, just before being announced, it helps enormously to take four deep breaths into the lungs, inhaling through the nose and exhaling via the mouth. This steadies the stomach muscles for it is in this region you usually feel the most qualms. So just breathe deeply and steadily – then rise to your feet. But keep good control otherwise you may find yourself huffing into the microphone and causing a gusty wind effect all over the room before you have even uttered a word.

Another tip in early speaking, especially if you are seated at a table, is to waggle your wrists loosely by your side to keep blood circulation going. Keep the hands out of sight, of course, or the audience may think you are preparing to do card tricks.

Nerves can be overcome by taking things slowly. A sure sign of the novice is when he leaps to his feet almost cutting off the toastmaster's announcement, and gabbles headlong into his speech, as if to get it over in record time to rush out to the toilet. One should, in a speech, speak slightly slower than in ordinary conversation. But do not drag it out, of course, carefully enunciating every word as if you are addressing a class of backward children. If you have a tendency to speak fast in normal life, you must take this characteristic into account on a public platform – and curb it. Otherwise nerves will make you speak even more rapidly and the result will be almost incomprehensible.

Knowing fully what you are talking about helps nerves too. If you have rehearsed your speech industriously, with all the salient points crystal clear in your mind and your notes on the table below you to save you 'drying', confidence soon ousts nerves with every succeeding word. But stand up uncertain of your speech format or your presentation of the subject and this additional handicap magnifies your feeling of insecurity. So give your nerves every chance by rising as near perfect in rehearsal as possible.

There are no short cuts to acquiring the nerve to speak in public – and, even if there were, the chances are they would give you a false personality. Some instructors have advocated yoga, auto-suggestion and even long-term exercises taking weeks of preparation. But, in my opinion, the more you delay your speaking appearance, the more tension you will suffer. The very fact that you are exercising over a long period to conquer nerves, makes them a hazard consistently more apparent! While such 'nerve-training' systems might suit minority metabolisms, the best antidote is to find yourself on your feet with an audience ready to listen to you.

Quite a few of us have suddenly been called upon at some social or business function and, before we have had time to dwell on nerves, we are up and spouting. While we might well eventually run out of steam when inspiration deserts us, it is by far the best sort of initiation. However not everyone has the luck to get off the ground that way.

The greatest easement of pre-speech tensions is the realisation that our shortcomings will receive sympathetic reaction from an understanding audience. It stands to reason. People want to be entertained. They don't want you ill-at-ease. And they will more readily forgive a nervous but subject-perfect speaker than a brash, over-confident bombast who is the wrong horse for the course – but doesn't realise it.

All stage, television and radio performers admit to nerves. If they do not they are either lying or lack real creative ability. I often quote the famous French star, Sarah Bernhardt, who confessed to a small-time actress that she felt nervous before an entrance.

'You, a great actress, nervous?' the girl laughed scornfully. 'Me, I'm never nervous when I go on . . .'

'Ah, ma cherie,' said the great star, 'but wait until you have some talent.'

It is the absolute isolation of public speaking which causes tension. We are speaking alone, ours is the only voice. There is none of the contrasting atmosphere of the pub, club or daily working hubbub to background our words. If we stopped speaking there would be a silence – and hundreds of quizzical eyes on us. It is moments like these when, after a falter, we begin, in effect, to listen to ourselves – and become scared at the enormity of our cheek in daring to stand up in the first place. Muscles tighten, our voice sails up two tones, we sweat and tremble. But if our speech is well prepared, we can press on and the stumble is soon forgotten as we regain control and repose.

And, if it is any consolation, even after thirty years of professional acting and public speaking, I still rise with niggling doubts and anxieties, which pass off as soon as I get under way. The reason is, that with thousands of public appearances in so many fields behind me, the more I know can go wrong . . . as a novice I did not know these snags!

Rising with a reputation to maintain, too, can be a strain, especially if you have a rather specialised audience in front of you. But, I repeat, most nerves are caused by being insecure in what you are going to say. Rehearsed familiarity with your speech cuts down tension by half and, once you find the audience is genial and attentive, your doubts disappear. And, when you sit down amid applause, you wonder why you ever questioned your own ability in the first place.

Stage fright is, however, quite another and more dreadful menace. Mostly we suffer it but once – not necessarily in our first speech but always early on in speaking careers. Perhaps the function is larger or more important than we envisaged when we accepted the date. We are suddenly faced with a situation seemingly beyond our capabilities. Then, for a few miserable seconds, we might get a feeling of near black-out, of total terror which disappears in a flash but leaves us rather frightened and even more uncertain. But it *does* pass – and rarely happens twice. And the more you can reassure yourself that you are the right horse for each particular course you tackle, the less likelihood there is of it every happening at all.

Alcohol and Drugs
Stage-fright can also be caused through taking pep pills or too many drinks before speaking. Often 'dutch courage' imbibed in the hope that it will give one a false personality to meet the occasion re-acts the other way and leaves one gibbering with terror, especially if, the alcohol has also been mixed with drugs.

Never rely on artifical stimulants of any kind to help you face audiences. At dinners and luncheons one is often a little wined up before one is called upon – I suppose it is fair to say that, unless a speaker is a teetotaller, no one on these occasions can ever be considered completely sober when they speak! But the experienced ones have, over the years, become accustomed to knowing their safe intake and so drink accordingly. Thus, never rely on alcohol increasing your word power or enlarging your image. If you should get the taste for drink, you will always need it, indeed suffer stage fright if you cannot get it. And if your firm asks you to address some important clients at 10.30 in the morning, you may not be able to slip out to a pub or raid the boardroom decanter. If you have become hooked on a drop of the hard stuff to see you through, you may well make mess of a speech when not so primed. And your speaking career will inevitably be a short one if it becomes reliant upon drugs or alcohol.

You do not rehearse with gulped brandies or pep pills and so, if you imbibe excessively on the night, you rise to speak in a form of temporary insanity. You have an exaggerated idea of your powers, are inclined to take risks which, in the cold light of day, you would never consider, especially with 'blue' jokes or snide references in dubious taste. Feeling 'high' yourself, you think the room is in a similar state and the audience is bursting for you to be witty and daring. So you go too far, offend or foul up some business deal. Ordinary nervousness is in itself an assurance that you won't take such chances. Drunks on their feet mostly repeat themselves and they never know when to stop. Many a good evening has been ruined by one lush speaker letting the organisers down by a rambling, semi-inarticulate discourse. Don't let it ever be you.

A glass of wine or two before you speak at a dinner is perfectly acceptable but an overdose of spirit or going on a pill trip will land you in dire trouble.

No drink or drug will ever give you talent.

Starting Small

Unless you are especially gifted or possess a superiority complex, which enables you to commence a career of public appearances by, in effect, playing Hamlet the first time you tread any stage, you must expect, as we all did, to start small. Few can begin as stars and those who try inevitably come to earth with a dull thud. Mistakes made by those professing to be at the top are not as easily forgiven as are the errors made by beginners short on experience.

So, to begin with, we may have to take a backseat during others' successes, but our hour will come. In the meantime we must read, mark, learn and inwardly digest other speakers and profit by study of their expertise, techniques, gimmickry – and even their gaffes and lapses from good taste! Lessons can be learned from them all if we are not too impatient to get the spotlight full on ourselves before we know the business. While it is a modern tendency to rush instruction in a desire to achieve 'instant success', let others show us a few mistakes first – then we will not make so many of our own.

However, take any chance your own particular world offers you to appear in public. Join a drama group, speak lines not your own to increase your vocabulary. Walk a stage – so useful in lecturing or in the demonstration-type talk when you may have to move between diagrams or models on a platform. Also learn how to stand still when speaking. And, above all, get used to projecting your voice clearly . . . even if you start by questioning your local M.P. from the body of a crowded hall.

See if you can assist in functions involving public speaking, campaigns and seminars. Move around in the atmosphere, even if you are not, as yet, on the speaking bill yourself. It is surprising the pointers you can pick up.

However, you must beware that, as you begin to find outlets for public speaking, you do not become over-confident. Every speech is a new adventure and, despite the many times you may have made it to other audiences, it will not always appeal in the same way. You have to ensure you know the right way –each time – by developing a sense of audience appraisal. And that is not acquired in a few days!

It is one hell of a task to conform to Polonius's advice to his son; 'to thine ownself be true', especially as that smug Lord Chamberlain hardly practiced what he preached, his good intentions constantly being swamped by self-importance. Which also sums up many public speakers . . .

The Value of Public Speaking

Speaking in public is vital for three reasons.

1. *The Community Spirit:*
By having the ability to communicate with mass audiences you can help with general education besides, in lighter subjects, bringing considerable pleasure and entertainment. Spontaneous 'live' personal appearances are in danger of having too few exponents, as witness that survey with which I opened my Introduction. Children see television before they meet a 'live' school teacher or see a real pantomime (if they ever do). Yet the flesh-and-blood contact is the real happening – it is not 'canned', pre-filmed or manufactured with all errors ironed out – it has the vitality and originality of taking place before your very eyes, with the audience actually participating.

2. *The Business World:*
Employers want men and women who can 'sell' to the public. Thus speaking to audiences is an essential qualification for most jobs. If you avoid the limelight, you just won't get noticed – and there are far too many in the dark cellars as it is.

3. *The Civic or Political Field:*
We have discussed the deprived citizens who are sitting ducks for the big guns of exploitation because they have no personal voice. One day they may rely on yours. Society as a whole wants more fearless, articulate speakers who can help those in danger of being 'taken over' through ignorance. Thus, as you

progress, you must move away from your own set. Standing up and preaching to the converted when you have the full support of the room is very pleasant but, to be really adept at civic or political hustings, you must be prepared to face strangers, especially those whose views are diametrically opposed to yours. And know how to keep your cool!

Summary of THE WAY AHEAD
1. Know yourself ruthlessly.
2. Be sincere – adjust yourself to your subject, not vice versa.
3. Polish up your vocabulary and grammar.
4. Use a thesaurus.
5. Study words that can be misapplied.
6. Avoid jargon in speeches.
7. The value of brevity and simplicity.
8. Know your limitations and use them to advantage.
9 . Use 'entertainment' in speeches.
10. The best antidote to pre-speech nerves is industrious rehearsal.
11. Avoid, like the plague, drugs and alcohol as 'dutch courage'.
12. Start small.

CHAPTER TWO

Your Voice

What type of voice do you possess? Tenor, soprano, baritone, alto, contralto or bass? Whichever timbre is your endowment, rich, gruff, shrill, dulcet-toned or gravel-harsh, high, low, flat or fog-horn, you will have to adjust to make the best of it. You cannot change your sound box. A deep voice might be unsuitable for a light-hearted subject whereas a woman's treble can sound just right. But, she, in turn, may be unconvincing when dealing with some sombre scientific study. Yet both these voices might, because of the brains behind them, have to cope with such subjects. So, in the long run, it will be your personality which counts.

H. G. Wells had a squeaky voice. Yet, once over the initial shock of his high pitch, his lecture audiences knew they were in the presence of a master. His mind was brilliant, his vocabulary vast and his knowledge a liberating influence for many. The reason those of us who were born too late to hear him know he had a squeaky voice is because it was often the only criticism his carping opponents could level against him!

So, if you suffer with similar vocal chords, do not despair. You can still get to the top provided you have good material to utter. It is the thought behind the words which gives them power, not superficial oratory. Some academic speakers with monotonous voices seem to deprive words of life and have to work extremely hard to impart their information. But others have a natural flair for cadence and inflexion which allows them to present the most ordinary dialogue in a colourful, interesting style. The words become not only significant of the speaker's character but imbue each subject with originality.

43

Often we hear a quotation, e.g. 'People ask you for criticism, but they want only praise' and when it is known that Somerset Maugham wrote it, his devotees say 'Typical of Willy'.

So your aim at the start is to be 'typical' of yourself. You must endeavour to reveal your true personality when you speak, suiting your voice with appropriate vocabulary – and getting an individual angle on your subject. It will be the novelty of your approach which will make you stand out from the ordinary ritualistic speakers, hide-bound by tradition or egotism.

You have a head start if you know your own language really well. When you learn a foreign tongue it requires long-term proficiency in its grammar, pronunciations and colloquialisms, before you could speak it in public. In fact you have to *think* in that language if you aim to be really positive. Public speaking in your own tongue means you begin by infusing your own thoughts and personality into your speech.

But, in turn, you must also treat your voice with respect physically.

Fitness

It is essential for a good speaker to keep healthy. We all know the misery of trying to communicate when handicapped by a sore throat or heavy head or chest cold. Experienced speakers can overcome these obstacles, usually by apologising to the audience in advance for their hoarseness which, in itself, shows confidence and repose. But it is no way to work if you can avoid it.

Before speaking in public a few good walks will tone you up. Mull over the speech in your mind with a dog at your heels. Take measured steps. Do not try to break any long distance records but breathe deeply and evenly all the time. Do not stroll; stride purposefully to exercise the muscles. If you are lucky enough to get away from highway fumes and find country or sea air (a lonely cove with a busy tide as your only audience is most exhilarating), you will reap a rich reward in chest expansion and head clearance.

If your mind and body are alert and well in tune, the rehearsals for speeches will not come as a chore. You will feel in the mood for them and the words will sink in quickly because your mind is itself creative and receptive. But if you are sluggish in health you can be sure you will only apply half your brain to the job. This, in turn, can lead to an over-anxiety neurosis to further drag you down. And, when you rise to speak, this can manifest itself in a form of aggression which has been defined as 'the arrogance of hyper-tension' ... you are so strung up that you attack the audience rather than woo it. Your tautened nerves make you assume your hearers are hostile when they are not, but they may well become so if rubbed the wrong way!

Such speakers are very embarrassing, especially on light-hearted social occasions. I remember at a harmless cricket dinner, R. C. Robertson-Glasgow whispering to me about such a belligerent speaker: 'You have to take what he says with a pinch of assault!'

Exercises in Breathing
The vital parts to keep in trim are the larynx and chest – although, of course, the whole body should be considered in public speaking. Even a sore finger can hamper full success. I have spoken, standing, one knee on a chair because of a football twisted ankle, but it did not make for repose.

But to exercise the chest we have only to remember what we were taught in the school gymnasium. Naturally, as some of us may not be quite as fit as we were then, start slowly, doing a little at a time. Then, as the body and muscles become once again familiar with the exercises, we can increase the duration of each one.

Stand upright, legs slightly apart, hands across the chest, palms downwards and finger tips touching, elbows slightly below the shoulder line. Fling arms wide, turning palms outwards as if telling a fishing story, and back in again.

In the same stance, jut arms straight out in front, palms inwards. Then fling them wide and back again several times, thus expanding the chest.

Finger tips of both hands touching behind nape of neck. Then twist the whole trunk from side to side.

Hold head straight and, with hands on hips, turn head right and left over each shoulder alternately to strengthen neck muscles.

Press-ups or any exercises which, by rotating the arms, expand and contract the chest are good for your lungs. Always breathe deeply throughout and stand straight. One must always, if possible, avoid any hint of round-shoulderedness in our speaking posture. You cannot obtain full power hunched up.

One could go into a lot of technical and biological details about intercostal breathing, the thorax etc., but that would only complicate the average speaker. All you need to know to speak well is the breath-control of an athlete, a good open chest, regular breathing and a relaxed mind and body. The exercises I quote I've seen practiced by Henry Cooper, once European heavyweight champion, who so very nearly proved Mohammed Ali had feet of clay. As Henry said, he still had to keep in trim even though retired from boxing as he was now making after-dinner speeches – which took more out of him than fifteen rounds in the ring!

Do not despise the old Victorian custom of 'opening the window and throwing out your chest'. Good, deep breathing in fresh morning air is most beneficial. You relieve the congestion of the night, clear the head, and such concentrated breathing stimulates the brain as well as the lungs.

Golf helps if the game is devoid of tournament tension. But, in the main, the long walk, breathing in fresh air, is far and away the best exercise. Fill the lungs, expand the chest, hold back the shoulders, inhale and exhale in a steady balanced rhythm as you pace with purpose.

If, prior to a speaking date, you do suffer from throat soreness – a lot of it can be psychosomatic of course! – a warm, honey and lemon drink, sipped rather than quaffed, is a relief. Some even like a dash of rum in it – but do make it a dash! Warm milk is soothing, too, just before retiring for the night. But never rely on neat spirit. It not only inflames the mind but also the already tender throat.

A tip when at dinners. If I am to speak I always avoid biscuits with cheese as these are flakey and apt to cause crumbs in the throat. I once rose and proceeded to cough like an avalanche after biscuits crumbs 'went the wrong way'. Of course the audience thought it hilarious – called it a 'crummy' speech – but it taught me a lesson.

There are several good throat gargles on the chemists' shelves but I always prefer the old remedy of half a teaspoonful of salt stirred into a cup of warm water. I always keep drinking water at my bedside. Not everybody needs it, indeed on cold nights it can keep you awake. But if your mouth has a tendency to dryness, especially with smokers, then just a sip of water, rolled round inside the cheeks, does help.

Breath Control

I mentioned in Chapter One that a good lungful of air helps the nerves when you are about to rise and speak. Nerves tend to make you breathe more quickly and therefore shallowly, giving the lungs little expansion so you lose projection power and emphasis. Sometimes you can so restrict yourself that you have not even enough wind left to reach the end of a sentence when the next good breath would normally be drawn. So, running out of puff, your voice drops to a half-strangled whisper and air has to be gulped in, shattering into pieces what would have been one fluent sentence.

When you stand to speak you should inhale through the nose and exhale from the mouth rhythmically. Then, once the upper part of the lungs are filled, you can rely on the abdominal system, the subconscious breathing we employ in ordinary life and when asleep. You don't have to think about that or, when speaking in public, ever be conscious of it. But when you reach a full stop or premeditated pause in your memorised script, revert to chest breathing once more and consciously inhale through the nose – not with a great heave of the shoulders of cause – and then resume the normal process again. Gradually, so uniform will this procedure become that you will not notice how well and regularly you are breathing.

Mark you, while I will deal with speech writing later, it is as well at this point to remember not to give yourself sentences far too long to sustain in one breath. When you set down a speech on paper you must mark breaks with commas, colons and full stops to cater for good breath intake and outlet. As singers breathe between bars of a song, so you will replenish your lungs at natural pauses in a speech.

Using Your Mouth

A fault with novice speakers during pauses or full stops is to leave the mouth open. The lower jaw is left sagging down, and is only brought up to form the words to begin the next sentence. This dries the mouth so that the speaker has eventually to suck up saliva or resort to a gulp of water. I have seen speakers literally stick their tongues out at audiences in a vain quest for moisture! If this happens *during* a sentence, say in the middle of a rising crescendo, an enforced pause inevitably kills the climax. So train yourself to momentarily close your mouth each time you reach a pause of full stop length in your speech.

However, when actually speaking, do *open* your mouth and use your lower jaw. It is the curse of some modern speakers that they seem afraid to show they possess teeth, true or false. They speak consistently through a slit in their lips or even through clenched teeth. Others let the words slip from the side of their mouths like a gangster tip-off. Many speakers, early in their careers, seem scared of using their mouths to advantage, indeed, seem half ashamed of speaking at all. They will even turn their heads away from the audience – and the microphone – as if pretending neither was there!

One must not over-enunciate, of course, but do form the tongue round the words, use the back of the teeth and the roof of the mouth. The letter 't' suffers a lot . . . so does 'd'. Both need the tongue, otherwise we get 'wone' for 'won't' and 'wonner' for 'wonder'. All this is alleviated by conscientious rehearsal.

Reading as an Exercise

Reading aloud helps a great deal. Take any newspaper account and pretend you are a newsreader. It is not as easy as that expert makes it appear but, with practice, and listening to others, you can achieve a very satisfactory balance of projection and clarity of diction.

Another good exercise is reading 'dialogue' aloud from a novel or play. See just how well you can time the lines, watch the pauses and study the punctuation. This, too, will allow you to experiment with dialects and characterisation, valuable if you intend to use anecdote in your speeches. Read to children too. This is also a good exercise in the handling of hecklers!

By reading aloud you become used to lifting your voice above normal conversational level, thus attuning your throat to a new projection without sudden strain.

Smoking

If you have not started – don't. But if you do smoke, discipline yourself to start later in the day than that fag before breakfast. And, on the day of the speech, lay off it altogether – if you can! I realise that for some a smoke does steady the nerves and I am not condemning them for that. Smoking helped many servicemen and civilians through the war when death in air raids was ever imminent and I would not criticise anyone for needing tobacco even now. It is far less of a vice than alcohol in the speaking world.

At a function do not smoke before you speak if you can avoid it. At dinners it is difficult, I know. Everyone round you bursts into flame after the dessert – or, more wretchedly, even after the soup sometimes – so that by the time you rise to speak the room looks like Smokey Joe's joint. But keep your own cigarette or cigar until after you have finished. Then it can be very satisfying and relax you after the ordeal. But light up before you speak and you may well gulp down smoke, become dry and parched and have to sip wine or water to clear the frogs from your throat during your speech.

Experienced speakers, of course, handle the smoking habit as they know best. They know their limitations, their nerve systems and their need. But, in the early days of speaking, you are far safer to abstain from smoking until after your speech.

Dentures

Consult your dentist. Tell him you have to appear in public and take his advice on the right adhesives if such are necessary. Also be certain that, before an engagement, you know exactly the right time to fix teeth to ensure security. Applied too early it can wear off, too late and the dentures will continue insecure. Above all rehearse with them, hear yourself on tape if you can and check for any sibilence. Not for nothing does the word 'siren' start with an 's'.

Teeth make such a difference to comfort in public speaking. I do not have to warn denture wearers to use a reliable fixative – and never use a public speech to test out new ones! Nothing

49

is more miserable than a plate slipping in the middle of a speech. At dinners when teeth have also been employed in munching, denture wearers are advised, during the break after coffee and before the speeches begin, to slip away, lock themselves in the loo and attend to any adjustments.

Personally I still have the misfortune of dentures ahead of me. At the moment my teeth, though long, are still my own. Even so I still like to use a toothpick, out of sight, now my molars lean like Stonehenge. But I deeply sympathise with anyone who, after years of public speaking with their own teeth, are suddenly forced to wear dentures. By hard rehearsal they overcome the change but many I know do take a little time out from the speaking round, to effect the transition.

I am reminded of the vicar who wore new dentures when preaching a sermon. Every sibilant 's' whistled through the church and the verger was kept busy shooing away dogs attracted to the vestry door. Later he advised the vicar to have his plate adjusted as the shrill sound had embarrassed the congregation, especially every time he mentioned the name of the Son of God.

The vicar saw his dentist and arranged for a new plate. A week later he returned and fitted it in. He stared into a mirror, opened his mouth and uttered: 'Jesus Christ . . . Jesus Christ . . .'

And the dentist snapped: '*Now* what the hell's the matter with 'em?'

If when speaking you ever have an obvious dental mishap, that story will get you out of trouble – if the audience is suitable, of course!

Voice Projection

You must learn to speak aloud in public without strain on the vocal chords. They are delicate membranes, capable of extraordinary power but only *if trained to do so*. Should you suddenly start shouting, in an erroneous interpretation of voice projection, you could stretch your vocal chords beyond their limits and be reduced to a husky whisper. And they do not heal easily from such maltreatment.

In early speaking days newcomers often meet this problem,

especially if they speak at somewhat gritty political meetings when they try and rise above bawling opponents. And they do risk damaging their voice, sometimes permanently.

I will talk about microphones later but, if you should be called upon to address a large meeting without one, the pitch you need is that with which you could call for order during a party or conference 'break' in a room already buzzing with conversation. You have, in effect, to make yourself heard over a group of people already making *themselves* heard over a background of chat. You do not bellow or roar – that would annoy those present who hate to be ordered about. No, you project your voice above the conversationalists, ringing and clear, still within your voice-box range but without imparting strain upon it. First-class toast-masters possess it – they never actually shout but raise their voices authoritatively.

Another good example is a cleric performing a wedding cere-mony. He lifts his voice so that guests at the back of the church can hear his words but he does not deafen the bride and groom in the process.

Voice projection is a sort of sixth sense you gain with ex-perience. With or without microphones you will be able to judge the carrying power of your voice to the back of every hall. Actors must have this accomplishment – so must public speakers. But you need to practice hard. Nothing is worse in a speech than inaudibility.

Although conversely, there is this story :

Voice from rear of the hall : 'We can't hear the speaker at the back.'

Voice from Row A : 'We in front are not so lucky !'

Elocution

This often disturbs future speakers as it conjures up a fantasy of fish-oval mouths, heavy exaggeration, 'ham' actor intonation, the flowery phrasing of would-be poets who speak, eyes closed, revelling in the sound of their own voices. I have heard several such over-trained speakers. Every word is uttered with an em-phasis more suitable to Greek drama than the church bazaar they are declaring open. They have no 'throw-away' technique, no deft asides or snap observations. Every word is ponderously enunciated in a stylised manner and quite innocuous statements

are given a ringing importance absurdly beyond their true value
– or the mood of the occasion.

A friend of mine read a book on speech improvement which
suggested he watched himself enunciate before a mirror. None of
us will ever forget his first speech. Intent upon mouthing every
word distinctly his mouth opened to form a chasm and the
speech was chanted out in a sort of march time rather than
spoken in a variable rhythm. He also wore a fixed expression
of intense concentration, eyes wide and staring, his mouth opening and shutting like a giant clam. The room was stunned for
a few moments then someone shouted : 'Who's doing the voice?'

That was it – a ventriloquist's doll! Being a showbusiness
occasion that interruption brought the house down. Our poor
friend sank down in despair. Rough treatment perhaps – but
now he speaks extremely well in public – and often uses that
story against himself in his speeches. We can all turn such
mistakes to speaking advantage if we keep our sense of humour.

But elocution is required in a modified sense regardless of
that daunting drama image. We must speak distinctly, with
correct projection, emphasis and inflexion, with proper breath
control and repose in delivery. There is no mystique about that.
Elocution is not just an academic exercise for an élite, it is a
natural process for all public speakers, a required achievement.
We must practise with the instrument we possess, a vocal organ
upon which we can play correctly.

While speaking 'correctly' is, I maintain, a matter of opinion
depending upon *who* is speaking, simple clarity is not. It is
essential. Precise elocution demanding complete grammatic
exactitude is a standard set by some text books. They are right,
perhaps, only that they must teach perfection in order to obtain
a high percentage of near misses like myself who can adjust
such instruction to suit our personalities.

But speaking, unlike science or mathematics, has no one
Q.E.D. answer. No text book can cater for the millions of
separate characteristics of students. The very act of speaking
constitutes communication which embodies, also, individual
argument, personality – and, above all, originality. Established
rules rarely suit creative, independent people. And most of us
today have no long leisure in which to perfect our speech in a
way to please connoisseurs. And some, busy earning money for

home and family, may feel there is a snob element in grammatical perfection. However, the academic message is fundamentally excellent – to be able to speak clearly. But ultra-elocutionists are apt to concentrate more upon vocal reproduction as a 'sound' rather than the medium through which we can absorb the thoughts of an inventive, imaginative mind.

Thus your aim is to seek clarity of diction in the way best suited to the facilities at your disposal. Most of us have to strike a line between high-brow ethics and our own instincts.

If you want an example of clear speaking and of supreme confidence, pause at a street corner and listen to the Salvation Army. They of course possess the ultimate in dedication few ordinary public speakers have, but one can learn even more from them than just their message from the way they address audiences. Few possess rich, dark brown oratical voices. Most of them have marked regional accents far removed from the so-called Oxford accent and they rely entirely upon simple vocabulary. Their work too involves them in some pretty gritty audience participation at times but their ability to speak clearly, concisely and without affectation in public is an example many of us can follow. They use showmanship, yes, the Sally Army was founded on it, but they are both entertaining – and sincere.

Pace
As mentioned earlier a beginner's tendency is speak too fast. Nerves seem to dictate that sheer pace will obviate blemishes. Hence a speaker begins to stumble over phrases through going at a pace in excess of that with which he has rehearsed.

A speech is like a piano sonata, varying in rhythm, slowing sometimes as you approach a big movement or change of melody, heralding it with some anticipatory pause, then sweeping on, increasing the pace to the climax of each particular section. So, in a speech, if you are relating an anecdote, you may quicken on the less vital or more obvious aspects, the explanatory 'asides', so to speak, but you slow up as you reach the 'punch line' so that the surprise or dénouement at the end is pressed home to the audience clearly and succinctly.

Comedy is always the one ingredient of a speech where sheer racing speed shows up at its worst. Unused to being a comedian, a speaker will rush his points, perhaps half-ashamed at his own daring and also in the completely misguided view that, regardless of how it is delivered, a joke will carry itself. It will not – as I explain later, it takes telling.

Pace, too, is often confused with animation. Speakers by quickening the pace think they are demonstrating vitality. It is the use of apt vocabulary and sheer simplicity that makes a speaker animated.

But one must also avoid, like the ennui it causes, the long 'funeral' oration type speech. Some speakers, taking themselves extremely seriously, dwell long and droningly on their words. Speaking too slowly makes for very quick boredom. Experienced listeners will be able to anticipate your next words and soon get well ahead of you! And when the monotony is no longer bearable, muttered conversation is heard under his flat voice. A lagging pace kills that element of surprise so vital in the entertainment of a speech.

In public speaking you do speak a degree slower than in ordinary conversation, remembering that your words have to travel further than just across a table or desk. So you do put the brake on your natural pace – but don't halve it or you can sound very dreary.

Clarity of Diction
Every word must be enunciated according to its importance, some with more emphasis than others, but *all* must be heard. Slurring words – or cutting them off short – are common faults which have to be overcome. Trying to be trendy or too colloquial can make for inaudibility, especially if the speaker is a little self-conscious in delivery.

The intrusive 'r' for example. *'Easy on your ear'* becomes *'easy on your rear'*. The overstressed 'g' when *'singing'* becomes *'sing-ging'*. Disc jockey's dialogue is not recommended for public speaking . . . *'going to'* becomes *'gunner'*, *'tomorrow'* becomes *'termorrer'*. *'Hours'* in some BBC commentators' phrase book becomes *'ahs'*. There is the dropped 'g', once the cult of the long-gone landed gentry, *'huntin' '*, *'shootin' '*, *'fishin' '*. *'And'* becomes *'an' '*, *'is he'* becomes *'izzy'* and *'please'* develops an extra syllable to become *'per-leese'*. And the Londoner may drop the 'h' in *' 'orror'* but put it back in *'h'angry'*.

A well-known Cockney M.P. in the 'twenties, once said to

F. E. Smith, later Lord Birkenhead, a barrister of scathing wit :
'I've gotta an n'orrible 'eadache' to receive the reply; 'Why
don't you take a couple of aspirates?'

In citing these common faults I quote them because they
cause inaudibility and confusion in public speaking. Only you
can train yourself in word useage according to what sort of
vocabulary you possess. I am forced to generalise for we are all
different. And some more different than others. Careless talk
will not inspire confidence in public. Speaking is not a lofty
achievement reserved for a blue-blooded class, it is a basic necessity for all mankind and only the downright indolent make a
fetish of poor speaking. A language is an inheritance and we
would be lost if deprived of it, so why not make the best use of
it?

Resonance, modulation – common-sense explains these necessary adjuncts to clear speaking. Light and shade to avoid a
monotonous tone, the inflexions on questions ... '*And what
have we got?*' '*Got*' is a high note, in effect, but emphasise,
instead, '*what*' or '*have*' and you get a different sense. Then
there is the drop in inflexion when you give the answer ... *A
completely new project altogether*'. '*New*' is the highpoint and
the rest of the sentence descends slightly down the scale.

It is all a question of logic and being natural rather than
the hypocrisy of using bad speech as a personal gimmick peculiar to yourself. It won't be – it will be all too common! And
keep you in a very low league of speakers.

Tone and Pitch

We all possess a natural middle tone. Some of us have higher
pitched voices than others with different middle registers, so do
not try and change this. Trying to affect a higher or lower tone
against nature and you can sound like a singer who has begun
in the wrong key. Sooner or later the range, either up or down,
will be too much for you. So you end on a cracked squeak or,
breathlessly grunting down in cellar cool.

Now, if you dare tackle it, singing is a very good exercise for
public speaking, even if you are not particularly musical. If you
can shut yourself away and belt out a few choruses you know
well, it will aid the rise and fall of your voice – and assist
phrasing as well. You will also adhere to the ballad's required

rhythm, matching the lyric syllables to the music. Never mind if you have a voice like a mother hen – just make sure the house is empty and let rip. And note how you draw breath between phrases. Mark you, the neighbours may want to choke it out of you – but it is all in the cause of art!

Another tendency to avoid at all costs is *'reciting'* a speech, an effect caused by learning a speech parrot-fashion. Nerves can cause this. You are so dead set on saying the lines that you concentrate more on getting them off your chest rather than put your personality into them.

One uses higher tones to simulate amazement, bewilderment, fright or even the querulousness of old age. Lower tones can be used for suspicion, doubt, acceptance and the 'asides' of a speech. The lower register can be 'placatory' and, if a modified resonance is used, make a deep impression on an audience. Deeper voice notes can infuse sympathy and compassion, provided you do not growl like an old-tyme stage villain. Always keep your tones as mellow as your own voice box allows and reserve the really high whine or low growl for versatile characterisation in anecdotes or jokes rather than part of your real personal style.

But lowering the voice can cause inaudibility. Beware the soft tone I term 'over-ripe' intonation when a speaker gets so carried away with pathos or sentimentality that he sinks to a whisper. One can never rely on complete silence in a hall or dining-room. If you aim to get an effect by a mere whisper, sure as fate someone will cough right on the vital line. So it is lost, so is the point you wanted to make – and you cannot repeat it. Not even a microphone can pick up your murmur if there is a sudden breakage in the adjoining kitchen or someone drops a glass in the audience.

It is always best to simulate a whisper in a speech if you should need one, rather than actually deliver it. Use of the hand at the side of the mouth can most effectively portray a mutter and allows you to use your normal voice only a shade down in tone. Nor need you shout if you are impersonating a sergeant major in an anecdote, just pitch the voice slightly louder than the normal you have been using. Always remember that whatever you may wish to convey in a compelling speech, its volume must always be easy on the ear of the audience.

Accentuation of Words

There are certain words which have different accentuation according to which pundit camp you belong. There is 'con-*trov*-ersy' or '*con*-troversy' for example but, provided either is right and the audience hears it loud and clear, it matters little. One strange affectation I recall from sports dinners in the past were erudite gentlemen who would refer to cricketer Denis Compton, in his presence, as '*Cump*ton'. He was in the Army with me and always called himself *Com*pton! So not even your own name is sacred ...

But there can also be stupid gaffes not only in pronunciation but in accentuation of words. Reason – we see them in print, glean their meaning from the context but never actually hear them spoken. We do not check which syllables are accentuated, we use layman's logic – and so mispronounce it. So for 'monotonous' the town mayor says 'mono-*tone*-us'. I have heard 'fatigew', 'indom-*mitt*able', 'inde-*fine*-ite', 'demon-*strat*-ive', even 'philoss-sopickal'! 'Architect' with the 'ch' sounded, become 'architeck' – and all the time the boys on the local press table are having a field day when such a speaker is on his feet.

These errors arise through trying to use words outside our normal vocabulary without checking them first. Take no chances with unfamiliar words unless you have actually heard them spoken by reliable conversationalists or have taken an expert's advice.

Repose, Rhythm and Pauses

Creative speakers gradually develop a rhythmic quality with experience. Your written speech must contain balanced phrasing – as I discuss later – so you have natural pauses of breath intake. One can begin a sentence rhythmically enough but, through lack of pauses, it will go haywire at the end through poor breathing opportunity in its framework, culminating in a sort of muffled aside. Rhythm means studying your commas and full stops.

Some speaker can use certain conjunctions 'and', 'but', etc., as miniscule breathing points, using slight pauses, sometimes most effectively. '*But* ... there *is* a danger in ...', so that a slight dramatic touch is infused by pausing after that first emphatic word.

Rhythm is often lost – and therefore timing, too – when a speaker either working without notes or, losing his place in them, gropes for a word he has forgotten. Let us say it is 'placid'. It does not come to mind so he attempts an alternative – and thinks of 'peaceful'. But just as he hits on that substitute, 'placid' returns to his mind . . . and the result is he may say 'peace-id'! In a life of speaking one hears some strange sounding word conglomerations . . . mostly by transposition of vowels or consonants and spoonerisms, the malformations usually being due to nerves or inadequate rehearsal. 'Grately deepful' was one of my early ones. Others I recall from taut speakers are Her Quajesty the Mean', 'the spevious preaker' and the famous radio spoonerism . . . 'music will be played from the Bath Room at Pump . . .'

Much of these errors were caused by rushing the speech. Never be afraid to use pauses provided they are not too long. They can be very effective, especially in instructional talks where you must make your points sink well home. Take this line :

'As soon as we have some time, we can build on it in our own image.' If you speak that too quickly, gabbling on to ignore the comma-pause, that sentence loses any profundity. Actually spoken by Sussex University mathematics lecturer, Dr Edward Gibson, he naturally gave it the correct rhythm and timing so that, on delivery, it became : *'As soon as we have some time – we can build on it in our own image.'* And his audience got the full impact of his message.

However no pause should be so long as to allow the audience to wonder if you have been struck dumb. The ham speaker who stares silently round the room, frowning and squinting to gain effect, often gets none. Long pauses are really only permissible in a speech when one has raised a laugh and the audience is itself filling the gap by participation. Here, of course, you must avoid talking into that laughter before it has died down sufficiently for everyone to hear your next remark.

Timing
In this sense 'timing' is not your speech length in minutes but how you deliver your material. It is involved with pausing and correct emphasis. As you do not speak into a laugh, nor do you

rush headlong from one aspect to another without giving your audience time to digest your previous information. 'Timing' means, in effect, that the audience hears *everything* you have to say to the N'th degree with just the right accentuation on each word so that all points are given their correct and relative proportion of importance. In other words – it is perfection!

Good timing is a gift. Some possess it naturally, others, even some most advanced speakers, still lack its true finesse – although they would not admit it. It is a stage requirement, but even then it is not by any means the accomplishment of all good actors. They reach a praiseworthy standard, of course, but few ever completely master this intricate talent. Basically perfect timing means that you extract one hundred per cent impact from all you say. You phrase, pause and emphasise on exactly the right syllables throughout without once sounding contrived or affected. Whereas all other attributes for good speaking may well be at an orator's command, 'timing' is sometimes ever so slightly awry on occasions. It does not always detract from the enjoyment of the speech, but, when near perfect, can add a new dimension and power to it.

It sounds daunting, but you may well find yourself blessed with the luck of in-built timing. It is a sort of sixth sense, taking every word at its right pace and being able to judge the strength of every sentence to gain the best result. It is not the speech you make that creates good timing, it is the form you are in when you deliver it. A slip of the tongue early on in a familiar speech can alter the timing considerably – so what was a riotous success with one audience will only go moderately well with another.

Most great stand-up comedians possess perfect timing as do actors of the calibre of Baron Olivier and Sir John Gielgud. In fact, the latter, when in Bombay playing 'Hamlet', once asked me to play him some Max Miller recordings, so greatly did he admire that comedian's expert timing. I must say the request shook me but I have remained inordinately grateful for what it taught me. Timing can be the result of a natural personality in a speaker. He feels at ease, nothing he says will land him out of his depth. The mind behind the voice is important. Nervousness and insecurity upsets timing but repose enhances it. Watch a television newscaster. Sometimes he is handed an item he has not seen before coming on the air. He reads it aloud – and it sounds exactly right, simply because natural timing is one of the main qualifications for his job.

Dialects

Whatever you do, never contrive to change your natural dialects. They are, sadly enough, dying out fast enough through the artificiality of some public speakers. A dialect is a personal possession to be cherished rather than scorned. If you are Yorkshire and proud of it, Texan and unashamed of it, it is no good trying to be Oxford or Boston. Never be tempted to 'put on' a 'correct' speaking voice beyond your own splendid, inborn inflections. This is where some speech courses tend to confuse students with natural brogues. They hear instructors enunciate and think that, to achieve such perfection, they must imitate. Quite wrong – as no doubt their instructors will tell them. Students must adapt the over-all teaching of speech framework but still retain their highly individual dialect.

I have known several people who adopt a 'false' voice in public speaking completely foreign to their natural timbre. On their feet they suddenly go 'all posh' and, if they have had a wine or two, always lapse disastrously back to their natural dialect half way through. 'Ad-libbing' usually causes it. They have carefully rehearsed their speech in their version of the 'Oxford' accent but are tempted away from the original script by some aside or inspired remark brought on by audience reaction. So they catch themselves off-guard – and back comes the home-town phrasing. And the audience giggle at the difference – which they would not have done had the speaker remained his true self.

Many sporting celebrities, finding themselves suddenly in demand as after-dinner speakers, fall into this trap. They feel they must sound 'educated' (their estimation of it, not ours) and, instead of the audience hearing a warm discourse from a much admired figure, they are treated to plummy tonsilitis. 'Mine' becomes *'main'*, 'line' becomes *'lane'* and the 'h' is sounded in 'honest'. So the cockney tries to sound like a 'landed gent' and the north-countryman an Ilkley Moor Noel Coward.

If you are a rustic, remain a rustic in you speech. You don't have to be the village idiot ... it is the content of your words that matter, not the dialect. So use it, promote it, publicise it, for it is as good as any form of speech from elsewhere. As it is, too many public speakers are cast in the similar mould of 'public school' speaking so it is a rare treat for audiences to hear a less familiar brogue. One has only to recall the splendid effect in wartime of Wilfred Pickles reading the radio news. The B.B.C. (too long the fashionable 'accent' criterion through no fault of its own perhaps), allowed the blitzed citizens to hear Pickles' warm Yorkshire vowels over the air and lighten a lot of darkness . . . especially when he made mistakes and corrected them with some typically jocular asides.

So always keep your speech identity. If you have any fears that, through nervousness, your personality alters too much when you speak in public, have a word with a candid friend. He, or better still, she, will advise where you go wrong. Listen to yourself on tape if possible and sort out any flaws. But bear in mind, always, that people come to hear *you,* not a caric-ature of yourself. Making a speech, as I said earlier in another context, is arduous enough without adding the burden of play-ing an entirely new role into the bargain !

The overriding importance of a speech is that the audience understand clearly what you are saying. Technique, dialect, gesture, tone, style are all strong assets but secondary to clarity of speech-content. Audiences would rather hear with clarity a technically imperfect speech which still conveys the right in-formation than a brilliant piece of oratory which takes a long time to say very little.

However, one warning with dialects. Always be sure that any colloquialisms or sayings peculiar to it are readily understand-able to those born outside your native boundaries. If in doubt, either explain them or substitute something else. We have to assess, quite cold bloodedly, that what we have to offer is not obscure to our audiences.

'Ums' and 'Ers'

The human voice is our greatest asset. It puts us above animals, not only in a communication sense but gives us a bond of interest in each other beyond natural reproduction – although that seems sometimes the only subject of conversation in which some humans indulge ! But we do waste lungfuls of breath in a lifetime with quite unnecessary 'ums' and 'ers'. These breed from a feeling that we must utter some sound even while thinking. We 'um', 'er', or qualify with 'well', just to keep the attention of the questioner, almost as if we felt he will run away if we do not have a pat answer. But it also denotes a lack of pausing ability, a form of insecurity. We feel we must keep the 'sound' going as well as the 'picture' although what we are filling the gap with is utter nonsense.

Some people just cannot speak, either in public or in normal conversation, without these echoes from the cradle. They often use more 'ums' and 'ers' than they do normal wordage. However difficult the task, it should be stamped out. It shows the brain and tongue are not in complete harmony and, while you are grunting 'um' or 'er', you are not leaving your mind completely free to consider the problem – so inevitable the answer is woolly, half-baked.

Listen to any television interview. It does not matter if the subject is a V.I.P. used to public utterance or the man in street, pressed for an off the cuff opinion . . . he or she will answer any query with . . . 'Well . . . er . . .' Once aware of it you can cut it out. You are asked a question, you want time to consider – so pause. Don't use up lung power with irrelevancies, especially to prefacing your answer with that exasperating gimmick – 'Now that's a fair question . . .' which always so obviously covers a very baffled mind! No audience wants to have to sort out the wheat from the chaff, so study economy in speaking so that *all* your words have weight. Use the thoughtful pause. It allows your voice and mind to be fully co-ordinated for your answer.

We have already discussed the 'didn't I?' qualification in dialogue but there are also the 'you knows'. Ladies, more than men, are inclined to seek your understanding by making public speeches, 'you knowing' all over the shop, seeking our reassurance in every sentence . . . 'I have to propose the health of our guest, you know. Well, he writes books, you know . . . Er . . . has travelled the world, you know. Um, oh, yes, we are pleased he is here tonight . . . er . . . he leads a very busy life, you know . . .' One longs to stand up and shout : 'We *don't* know, madam, that's why you're here to tell us . . . !'

If a computer could add up all our completely banal and

useless phrases we use per day what a terrible strain on lungs and larynx it would reveal! It would also magnify the shallow thinking behind daily dialogue. Some minds are too busy with minnow thoughts all darting about without ever being able to concentrate fully on any single subject under discussion. Lots of people live their whole lives in this way. Tell them someone is dead and they pull up with a jerk, struck dumb. Their minds are not tempered to such magnitude of thought. So they gasp, recover – and trivia takes over again.

Not their fault, of course, but education must seek to instil most positive thinking into speech. The vocal chords and the brain must be so related, each to be able to cope with the demands of the other in harmonious collaboration.

Tape Recorders

Hear yourself on tape always if it is possible; if you feel you are addicted to 'ums', 'ers', 'you knows' or my horrible fault, 'ah', with which I tend to preface replies in conversation, listen to your speech played back to you. It can be a dismal experience but well worthwhile. Few of us are ever completely devoid of speech idiosyncrasies, but being aware of them is a great step forward.

Put your early speeches on tape and listen to your enunciation, rhythm, timing and pauses – and hope, too, that you cannot hear yourself breathing too heavily into the bargain. You will be able to spot hesitances, loss of strength when you sound more querulous than secure, and soon you can get a very clear idea of how you are progressing.

We do not sound, on tape, ever as we think we do because the structure of the ear does not allow us to receive more than a cavernous echo of our real voice. So, if you have not heard yourself on record, it can come as a bit of a shock. Tape recorders are also useful in speech learning as I mention in Chapter Five.

Summary of YOUR VOICE
1. Use your voice in conjunction with your personality.
2. Keep fit. Exercise like an athlete.
3. The need for good regular breathing.

4. Reading aloud as an exercise.
5. Care of dentures.
6. Voice projection without strain.
7. Study of elocution generally to include clarity, pace, tone, pitch, rhythm, repose and use of the pause.
8. Timing.
9. Use natural dialects.
10. Avoid all speech hesitances, mispronunciations and lazy speech.
11. Use of tape recorders to hear flaws in speech.

CHAPTER THREE

Material and Forms of Speech-Making

Probably your first speech was, or will be, compiled against the clock. Perhaps you had to replace some other speaker unable to attend at the eleventh hour. So you had to scramble around for material, writing jokes from helpful friends in the cash columns of your diary and searching the library for quotations. This pressure is often the cause of additional nervousness for the newcomers to speaking. There is insufficient time for adequate rehearsal or research before the function. But, rushed or not, at least a start has been made.

Enterprising speech-makers continue collecting items all their lives. They do not rely on a haphazard memory bank; they use a meticulous filing system. I advise you to do likewise. Never be without a notebook in your briefcase, pocket or handbag. And, each evening, transfer your daily collection to your own files. Some use indexed books, others box files or card indexes. Whichever system you devise for yourself, label each receptacle under various headings which are liable to crop up in your speaking world . . . 'Humour', 'Quotations', 'Personal Anecdotes', 'Anecdotes of Famous Personalities', 'Money' (which crops up in most speeches along the line) 'Community References', 'Hobbies', 'Sport' – and others you know you will come to need for your own more specialised subjects.

A regular public speaker collects material like an ardent philatelist posts off first-issues to himself. Everything from share prices to wisecracks is filed away, the useful and the seemingly trivial information, and often the latter is used more than the former! But as he progresses up the speaking graph and widens his public so he will increase his fund of material. Stories abandoned in the early assays on the speaking world as 'flops' are often revived, rehashed and refurbished to be highly successful in the light of a greater understanding of the game.

So note down anecdotes of famous people you hear or read in all media, newspapers, journals, biographies, novels and even keep dated clippings to file under their respective headings.

You also file away, too, the notes you make for any one speech so that, if you are asked to make a return date, you can look up what you said last time and avoid repeating any items again. This ensures that you don't sound like a 'one speech' type – a danger which older speakers often fail to see. Too busy to prepare anything new, they rely on a stock speech which is only sensible if they are speaking to completely different audiences each time. Mostly with old age they are restricted to one locality and are prone to forget that their one highly amusing or successful speech has been heard by the same community many times.

Never be a one-speech maker. Experiment as you gain experience and widen your material all you can. I achieved it by making a similar speech to widely diverse audiences to begin with and then broke it up into three equally acceptable speeches which did not overlap each other in any way. By use of additional new material I was able to have three balanced scripts at my disposal should anyone ask me to come and speak again.

Initially, speakers are apt to put all their eggs in one basket but they will find, as they mature in speech-making, they will ration out their material. That is why a newcomer, having 'scored heavily', as the local press always say of successful speakers, may return the next year and be tame by comparison. He has either run out of ideas or cannot change his tack. Maintaining a standard is just as hard as making a start.

So train your mind to absorb speech material. It demands a more specialised viewpoint beyond the normal round. Memory is in itself a filing system which is rarely, if ever, over-used. With really old folk the storage space is sometimes filled up, hence they can recall their dim past with clarity yet completely forget what happened yesterday. The simple fact is there is no room left for yesterday. But, with the young, there is a vast tank which can be topped up with fresh supplies daily. So the mind needs developing like the voice or the hand-and-eye co-ordination of the games player. The mind will not work for you just because you possess it. You have to train it on the lines you want it to work. You will never make a good speech if you are lazy in acquiring knowledge or are incurious about other people.

So keep your ears and eyes alert, and your mind toned up, to all that goes on around you. Actually this thought process makes long distance travel, for example, far more interesting, certainly in public transport. Cooped up alone in a car for hundreds of miles does not give a speaker as much opportunity to broaden his or her vision as those who can rub shoulders with the community at large. Admittedly there is more bad temper about than there was, but at least the ordinary commuter is in the thick of things and therefore more like to hear opinions and get the feel of the world in general than those travelling alone.

If in your railway compartment there are three or four people who are not prepared to talk (much better if they do as you can always learn something from strangers) – then sit back and, without staring at them too searchingly, make up in your mind a story involving them all. Relate them to each other if you like, marry them off if necessary, but spend the trip working out a plot in which they play some sort of character, hero, heroine, villain or comic. I know it sounds crazy but it does exercise the mind to think creatively. You don't have to be a writer to do this, just use your imagination. A lady speaker I know often uses this travelling ploy. She tells me she only has one plot but she can weave it round any group she sees so that the different characters alter the story line every time. She obtains enormous amusement out of it – but will not tell me the plot!

Memory is a matter of paying attention to what goes on round you – and remembering, too, that you, yourself, are part of what goes on around other people. Too many citizens sidle through life as if they were the only one God cared about and, subconsciously, act that way. It is a strange trait. They seem certain that if they are not present at any event, then it does not matter and is of no interest to them. This self-centredness breeds a frustrating loneliness and such oddities never make good public speakers – although some of them try.

You will notice that such isolated people possess no sense of humour. Most self-styled hermits are incredibly vain people,

67

covering inferiority complexes, with a high-minded disdain for their fellow men. They will certainly never provide you with material for speeches!

You must be a good mixer. Be on the *qui vive* for apt remarks, odd wisecracks in pub or club and especially children's or young people's sayings. If used relevantly in a speech an 'out of the mouths of babes' quotation is almost always a sure-fire success. One true one that came my way was a child who had just learned the facts of life and gazed in wonderment at her mother: 'To think,' she said, 'you let a great brute of a man like daddy do that to you just to get me . . . it must have been awful for you.'

Always beware of using jokes heard recently on television or radio – or any story current 'doing the rounds'. Otherwise you can be left stranded without a good finish to your speech if a speaker uses it just before you stand up. It has been my bitter experience. Having woven a gag into the fabric of the speech to make it relevant, someone has used it in the preceding speech and I have been reduced to hasty improvisation, not good for the nerves. I now avoid that hazard by using anecdote rather than the isolated joke.

Harvest material all you can. My box files are labelled Commerce, Sport, Ladies Nights, Stag Nights, and the special headings within my own bohemian spheres, Television, Stage, Writing, Films, and so on, because I do a lot of speaking in show-business fields. Your groups, however, might well be Insurance, Advertising, Mechanics, Art, Music, Literature and, for ladies, Fashion, Cookery, Children, and – aye – Women's Lib.

It may sound as if you need to open an office in your home. Well, if you have the space, it is not such a bad idea. At least take over the spare bedroom between visitors. A retreat is not only good for writing speeches but learning them as well. You do need plenty of quiet for the necessary concentration.

Make Sure of Your Facts

No public speaker can risk being careless in research. So do not work purely on hearsay or tenth-hand information. Always check. It is all too easy to chance your arm that some gossip or rumour is true and then find yourself having to make an abject apology or, worse, sued for slander. It is surprising how many even well-qualified speakers make gaffes because they have not bothered to check their source of information. For example . . . I have heard this; 'As Churchill once said : "What the people want is information" and a voice from the audience snarled : "That wasn't Churchill, it was Northcliffe . . ."

At once that speaker lost respect. His authority was in question for the rest of his speech and he was treated with guarded suspicion from then on.

Then again, even if you have got your facts right, are they entirely relevant to the subject? Will they sound bad taste or cheap simply because you have dragged them in beyond the real brief for your speech. It is a nauseating habit of politicians to do this, by including some extraneous bitchiness or snide aside of party warfare, only remotely connected to the speech theme. My main quarrel against using *any* speech to stir up disquiet outside the relevant theme is that such speakers are arrogant enough to think audiences sufficiently sub-standard to accept it without question. The axiom of all good speech-making is to stick to the point. If you are proposing the health of the bride and groom you should not mention the Red Menace under the bed!

One simple courtesy that so often eludes speakers is getting names right. If you have to mention a stranger to you in a speech do check his name thoroughly and write it down. Sometimes when menus are hastily compiled with speakers' names accepted by phone rather than by the far more sensible letter, a name can be mis-spelled or even its pronunciation be obscure.

The late Gilbert Harding, television panel game star of the fifties, was a speaker always in great demand and I found myself on several bills with him. He had a belligerent yet highly intelligent and witty approach to life. And at one dinner he was introduced by a casual chairman was 'Mr Har*dinge*'. As Gilbert was then already a well-known public figure, the error was unforgivable and, as he had his critics, I have often wondered since whether it was done intentionally to infuriate him, or was just a stupid idea of a joke. However, Gilbert Harding was not a man to let it ride. He rose, puce in the face and, staring at the inept chairman, said : 'Sir, my name is Har*ding* – not Har*dinge* – but I can well understand how the word 'dinge'

69

crops up in a mind such as yours . . . I will now *singe* for my supper . . .'

It was a turbulent, strained night. But he had a point although, as always, he wrote and apologised for his rudeness the next morning. But I doubt if that guilty chairman effected the same courtesy.

If you are unsure of a fact and cannot trace its source, leave it out. Better safe than sorry. As I mentioned in the Introduction, I had to apologise in public once. The secretary of the club at which I was speaking had wrongly briefed me. He told me that the proposer of the toast to which I was replying was a family man. I had all the facts so I mentioned his wife and children but, unknown to me, they had changed the speaker – and the replacement was a bachelor! While it raised a laugh, it was an embarrassing experience – and partly my own fault. I should have noticed that name of the speaker on the menu was different from one notified me in the secretary's letter – and the change in the introduction.

Use your local library too. Research for one item so often leads to knowledge of others which can be used in subsequent speeches. For instance when commercial TV used as a soap powder slogan 'whiter than white' I discovered, when looking for something entirely different, that it had been said before – by Shakespeare! Yes, in 'Venus and Adonis' I read; 'teaching the sheets a whiter hue than white'. This quotation has served me well in speeches which needed an advertising reference.

One can buy books of quotations which are less likely to be familiar to audiences as the bon mots used on television. The apt 'quote' is always valuable. Remember too you cannot make amusing or enjoyable speeches if you are not abreast of the times. Older folk might, of course, but they usually work on comparisons between past and present which can be very diverting – and instructive.

You will only limit your speaking powers if you neglect to feed your brain with new material. Most of us like to think we are creative and possess highly original standpoints. But, sadly, as we grow older we are inevitably disenchanted to find that we are, in reality, very much like so many other people – and infinitely inferior to a good many, too, if we ever deign to admit it. So only by stimulating our minds can we hope to keep pace and such a valuable discipline it is that it could change our whole life and outlook.

Keeping To Your Allotted Time

In gathering material one must be prepared to prune it too. The bane of all speech-making functions is the speaker who goes on too long. He doesn't think so, of course, but you in the audience do and, as the customers on the receiving end, you are right. Think back to any speaking function you attended – always at least one speaker outstayed his welcome. These long players are the curse of organisers who plan an evening to a tight schedule only to find their speakers letting them down by exceeding their time allowance.

If you are allotted ten minutes, then speak for ten minutes. If an evening is designed for, say, cabaret or dancing to follow the speeches, then it is paramount that speakers stick to their time. No sane speaker can expect to hold an audience beyond a reasonable period if they are itching to watch a cabaret or dance.

I cannot stress the time rule too strongly. Speakers get carried away and, even if they have been circumspect in their timing at rehearsal, one laugh or burst of applause on the night and they feel the audience cannot bear to part with them! Vanity takes over. Off they go, at tangents – the 'that reminds me' technique, usually when the next remark is in actual fact a *non sequita* – and *ad lib* on well past their time limit. The following speakers naturally resent it, having likewise been limited in time allotment. So they break the rules, too – and from an animated brisk start the evening falls away into dreariness. I have heard speakers exceeding their time and doing very well, entertaining their audiences right royally – but with the room emptying all the time as people left to catch last buses and trains, most of them angry and frustrated at missing something good that should have been put on earlier.

Sometimes a special speaker is expected to be on his feet for three-quarters of an hour. If the highlight of a dinner is a big speech from an expert in his field, then the organisers must plan it that way. But usually they engage a few preliminary speakers who, not content merely to support the V.I.P., actually go all out to steal his thunder! Would-be comics will tell long rambling jokes before a star comedian stands up to entertain. These time hoggers never succeed in outshining the experts because their fundamental approach is wrong. Beyond the normal courtesies the audience is not there to hear the supporting speakers. Yet at least one will fool himself that he can impress beyond his limitations. Limelight hoggers can be a nightmare at a function. Choirboys when bored by a sermon once used a disgusting term for such time-stealers . . . verbal diarrhoea.

Always leave your audience wanting more – but never give it to them! The greatest compliment you will get is when a member of the audience tells you after a speech that 'I could have listened to you all night.' He couldn't, in actual fact, but he means that you really whetted his appetite with your fare, you were in good form and entirely relevant to the occasion.

Chairman should always call a halt to a gasbag speaker . . . tactfully of course, but firmly, however indignant they look. A speaking list is a team, but some members of it may feel slighted that their wit and wisdom is not considered worthy of more than ten minutes. So they arrive at the function quite determined to ignore any time limit, regardless of the organisers' arrangements. And go on to completely upset them. However hesitant or nervous a speaker might be – if he or she sticks to that one golden rule of obeying the time limit, they will be asked again. And everyone will want to encourage them.

Over-running is of course not only harmful to a speaker's reputation, also wasteful of material. Speakers usually find points for speeches hard enough to get and even jokes have to be sifted like gold dust. Using it all up in one marathon of a speech is plainly unintelligent because, once you exceed the normal time, the audience will become too bored to concentrate further, especially if you are keeping them from the bar and you are eating into a special extension time! Yet some speakers use up everything they know all in one tedious speech, as if it is going to be their last. And very often it is!

So, when you select material and plot a speech on paper, do so with the time limit foremost in your mind. No one minds the odd minute or so over the odds, especially if the extra time has been absorbed by gales of laughter between the spoken words. But make sure you actually deliver a speech timed according to your brief.

Copyists and Plagiarism

At a dinner a doctor told an uproarious story about a hospital operation. Another doctor next to me whispered: 'He wasn't even there . . .'

'How do you know?' I asked.

'Because it happened to *me* – not him.'

'Are you going to tell him?'

'Good God, no,' he hissed, 'he's senior to me!'

Many speakers are guilty of this form of plagiarism. I have often heard the same *bon mot* echoed by three different speakers at three successive functions all swearing that they 'were there at the time'. And each presented it with that smug, knowing look implying that he created it. All such speeches are in fact just pot-pourris of other speakers' efforts, gathered feloniously over years of going to dinners armed with a pencil and paper. Sometimes these copyists use the backs of menus for their 'cribs' – if I had my way they would print them in white lettering on all black backgrounds to stop this practise!

Sometimes these non-creative speakers are usually so busy writing during a speech that some speakers have been known to stop and ask if they are going too fast for them! But they have thick hides. They are out for oral plunder and only listen to other speakers in a looting frame of mind. I don't have to tell you to avoid this practise if you want to remain popular. You must cultivate your own imagination, not rely on other's.

There is no copyright on jokes of course. They are anyone's for the picking but there is, as I have said earlier, always the risk of too popular ones going stale on you before you rise to speak. Always have, if there is this risk, a few reserve jokes at the back of your notes in case you need a last minute substitution. But do refrain, when your time is up and you have not needed them, from *adding* them to your prepared speech and so steal part of some other speaker's time.

Anecdotes, too, are not copyright but often they can, ethically, belong entirely to certain speakers, especially if based on their own personal experience. If you should want to use them, then do acknowledge them to their rightful owner; never try to pass them off as your own.

I often use, especially on ladies night, a true incident which happened to me. After landing a B.B.C. contract some years ago I celebrated along with others in the show rather too well. During the evening I met veteran singer, Turner Layton, once famous in my extreme youth as part of the Layton and Johnson music hall act, and a firm favourite of my wife's family who had collected their records. So, to placate my wife when I arrived home rather late, I obtained Turner Layton's autograph on the reverse of a visiting card. In the early hours I tottered home and tried to explain why I was late. But alcohol had taken control of my tongue. I could only utter gibberish and my wife looked at me from the bed in utter amazement. So, as if to solve the problem, I remembered the autograph and showed it to her across the bed. Seeing only the visiting card my wife said; 'There's no need to show me that – I know who you are.'

That true story inevitably gets a good laugh because it is a human, domestic situation, ideal for community audiences who can identify themselves with such a situation. But one day I was at a dinner when a young man recounted it as happening personally to himself. But he did not even have the sense to alter Turner Layton's name to, say, Tom Jones. It was quite obvious to everyone in the room the speaker was far too young to have ever heard Turner Layton sing – let alone meet him! The story went absolutely flat simply because the room knew the boy was lying. But that anecdote has been constantly 'lifted' and at one time my wife used to carry the autographed visiting card round in her handbag as proof of authorship!

You will never make someone else's personal experience sound really effective when you twist it into your own. The fact that they created it gives them a head start . . . for they really see the truth in their mind as they tell it. So acknowledge any other speaker's anecdote – if you must use it all. But much better, tell your own.

Where copyist speakers fall down is their failure to obtain a true assessment of their own ability. They hear some practised speaker relate an hilarious anecdote and in their tiny minds they feel that it is also right up their street. So at the next opportunity they rise and tell the same story – only to lay an egg! Not a titter is raised and they can't think what has gone wrong.

Well, in the first place, the original speaker probably used the anecdote in a far better context than the copyist who tried to force it in merely for its own sake. The creator, too, cannily paved the way for it by subtle build-up, while the copyist just dropped it in baldly. Obviously the anecdote suited the creator's style – but not the copist's, on whose lips it sounded foreign and suspect. And another reason for the flop could be that the occasion was not right for such an anecdote and, even had the originator been on his feet, he might well have omitted it for certain types of audiences. The poor old copyist is, sadly, very rarely the right horse for any course! And those he does tackle he inevitably puts the cart in front . . .

By using other speakers' material you lay yourself wide open to criticism because, especially at business lunches and dinners, the most popular speakers are well known to a wide audience. And a quiet nudge indicates that the speaker has cribbed from a popular raconteur and possibly a career is drastically changed. The very fact that the speaker has copied another shows a contentment with the second-hand or a laziness in approach to a speech. We must learn to create our own scenes, not steal others and thereby drop bricks on our own toes.

Plagiarism is a common crime in the speaking world but most of the small-time operators get sorted out sooner or later in their lives. I know from experience – I have had whole speeches of mine put on tape unbeknown to me – and trotted out else-where, *word for word*, as some pirate's own life story!

Self-Intrusion in Speeches

You will note I closed the previous paragraph with 'life story' . . . but I would not, if I wanted to please some audiences, always use that personal sort of approach. If the occasion was a light-hearted one then you would be justified in taking *your* personal angle on it but if you are opening a charity fête your speech must primarily exhort the public to spend in a good cause. But quite often the VIP selected for such onerous jobs prattle on about themselves (or their Party!) throughout the whole opening ceremony and forget or ignore the hard work of the organisers or, most importantly of all, the REASON for the function.

On such occasions you must blend your personality with the event, not use it merely as a backdrop to your autobiography. However, if you are diligent in collecting material, you may well find some anecdote about yourself that will illustrate the charity or theme of the speech in a most natural way. But other occasions may present you with new pastures in which any personal data could be quite out of order.

We must always be prepared to take a back seat when either the more informed are at our elbows or when 'plugging' ourselves is completely irrelevant to the central theme. Sheer force of personality will not mask our ignorance of some finer points under discussion. And going where angels fear to tread often ends in fiasco. But, as a nine-year-old boy said to me once: 'Why do angels have to tread at all – they've got wings...' I gather now he is a young speaker very hard to match at his university.

Speeches at Social Functions

You have been asked to say a few words at a local dinner. It may well be your first-ever such invitation but, even if you have tackled the job before, it still needs planning with architectural thoroughness if you are not to let yourself down. Living within the community any gaffes on your part could haunt you round the town for many weeks afterwards! A stranger could flop and be forgotten in a few hours but when local boy or girl fails to make good, they find it hard to live down.

You may have had an unexpected success at your first attempt in your own social sphere and feel that there is nothing to this speech-making lark. It's a doddle, a piece of cake. First speeches are often successful because you are already well known to your audience. An occasion like your sports or social club dinner provides anyone local with a proven format into which they can fit without much stress. The local comic might even get away with a hotch-potch of stories unrelated to 'the toast of the guests'. His own circle might fold up with glee at his self-assurance. But that could set a dangerous precedent for his self-esteem.

We have to consider speaking publicly in its broadest sense

... not to an audience of sympathetic friends but standing up and trying to convince a roomful of strangers. They will not accept disjointed jokes – they do not want a club 'act', they want a 'speaker'. When you can impress people who have never seen or heard of you before, only then can you consider yourself a practised speaker.

Many a self-alleged comedian feels that sudden chilling shudder as his tommy-gun delivery of gags, the highlight of his own club suppers, falls on the silent, stoney ground of an unfamiliar audience. Where is the hysterical weepings of his cronies now? But the stern faces remain unyielding. They expect a different standard – they want a *relevant* speaker. They are not necessarily averse to laughter, but the humour must be part of the subject. Only professional comedians might get away with unapposite jokes – but even they sometimes fail to please more discerning audiences who want to hear about their jobs rather than act as 'try-out' guinea pigs for their latest jokes.

With local affairs topicality is always a winner, so search the district's newspapers. You know the local scene, so play upon it, make them laugh at themselves if you can. By all means use jokes but adapt them to suit the occasion. I deal with this in detail in Chapter 6. Certainly aim to amuse them if you can. Some parochial functions can be very dreary, as when the captain of the sports club reads out the past season's record like a railway time-table or madam chairman introduces a guest speaker so gravely, as if in awe of him, that it takes him half his speech to get the audience back off the floor from boredom. But just because the district of your speaking date has a problem about drains or motorways, the tennis club dinner/dance is not the place to air such grievances. Many a speaker gets very angry indeed when he can get no response from the football club for his haranguing of the council about its housing programme. Most likely he will get heckled. People attend such functions to be entertained – not brain-washed.

But the social occasion should present you, in early speaking days, with the least difficulty and is an ideal audience with which to start. You have a sympathetic audience when you stand up. The organisers have selected you because of your suitability to handle the speech. Your theme is crystal clear and you know what is expected of you.

77

In compiling the speech, too, you have contact with those in charge so you can discuss points with them. Indeed, with beginners, it is wise to do so. At least if anything did go wrong then those in authority know you did your best.

Facts must be double-checked of course, especially in cases where you are going to refer to other guests. You may even be able to chat it over with them personally. They will be flattered you are taking so much trouble – and can avoid moments like this:

Speaker: 'I well remember our honoured guest appearing at this dinner three years ago with his charming wife. She played the piano for us brilliantly then – and we welcome her again tonight . . .'

Neighbour (aside): 'He divorced her two years ago . . . this is a *different* wife . . .'

Poor research has lead to a terrible embarrassment for all concerned, a 'clanger' remembered against the speaker for ever in a small community. And imagine yourself in the shoes of that guest of honour. In his speech following he has to mention his new wife as she is present – but must also ignore the ill-chosen reference to his former musical mate who ran off with the insurance man.

So start social speaking in your home town but always remain aware that friends are easier to win over than strangers. Don't let local praise make you over-confident . . . because you have not been fully tested yet!

The Commercial Speech
Save for a memorial service address, possibly the most difficult of all. And the two often have a lot in common! It is never easy to make business speeches entertaining. A top man could, by dint of privilege and experience, indulge in some by-play perhaps but, in the main, any hint of facetiousness (or even true wit sometimes!) could be considered *de trot* if it in any way obscures the selling points of the project. Fun and games at the expense of a vital sales message could mean you would never be entrusted with such a speech again. Yet you must sound enthusiastic without being light-hearted. This is where your own personality counts.

Plotting such a speech is best achieved by sticking to a basic

78

principle of dividing the paragraphs, alternating stark fact with interesting relief – fact, interesting aspect, fact, interesting anecdote relevant to that fact, back to fact again – and so on. All that 'interest' with which you cushion each stark fact must be relevant, of course, although a smile or two, here and there, is permissible provided you are sticking to your point. Once you obviously digress, as if tired of your theme, you are saying to your audience, in effect, 'this is dull stuff so now watch me be funny', you may get your cards at the end of the week! You must never catch a business audience 'on the hop' like that. They have come to hear facts, they have conditioned themselves to that special mood of reception when, suddenly, they are faced with a bizarre approach to the subject which defies full concentration upon it.

Yet that same audience likes a real personality delivering such a talk. They feel in safe, authoritative hands. But if that personality or character is bigger than his subject, he is the wrong horse for the course . . . the audience will be studying and weighing *him* up rather than the object of the exercise.

Many firms try to stimulate speech-making acumen by sending their employees on special courses in the art. Always they are excellent value, especially for those who lack courage initially to stand up at all. Certainly these courses get them off the ground! But, in my humble opinion, some courses insist on a certain stylised form which does restrict the more vibrant personalities in the student groups and even proves a handicap when they face a wider range of audiences beyond the commercial fields.

I know many speakers who, after commercial speech training, have completely lost their original freshness and animation. Where once they were vital and witty, they seem to have had it all knocked out of them and now make even a toast to the bridesmaids sound like a ponderous commercial. Others, because they had to adapt an inherent racy style to suit their precise tutors, now only succeed in sounding like 'con' men in a street market. Over-emphasis of salesmanship can play havoc with some very bright characters.

American actor Joseph Jefferson wrote towards the end of the 19th century: 'Many instructors in the dramatic art fall into the error of teaching too much. The pupil should first be allowed to exhibit his quality and so teach the teacher what to teach. This course would answer the double purpose of first revealing how much a pupil is capable of learning, and, what is more important, of permitting him to display his powers un-trammelled, whereas, if the master begins by pounding his dogmas into the student, the latter becomes environed by a foreign influence which, if repugnant to his nature, may smother his ability.'

Only an old-school declamatory actor whose ancestor had performed at Drury Lane 200 years before could write that! But Jefferson's message still holds good today, both for actors and public speakers. While you must know the ropes of the job, they mustn't strangle you. Your natural voice must match your true personality, you have to develop a correct image – but you should be guided according to what you possess, rather than forced like a hot house plant.

It can be that some proficiency courses or text books put some students off. By their very highbrow presentation they sometimes assume that every student starts with some sort of academic 'know-how'. One girl told me that she felt she could never speak in public because she had a country accent and all guides she ever read seemed to insist on the Oxford accent. They didn't, of course – but the treatment of the subject indicated ultra-intellectualism.

Speech training courses whether internally organised by a company or by hired instructors, almost always work on a competitive system. The students discuss each other's faults – a good idea at the time – but it can mean that the rivalry in-stilled for commercial salesmanship becomes later misapplied in general public speaking. I know many efficient speakers today who would be even better if they did not regard all other speakers as antagonists to be put in the shade by superior talent. They would rather be the best of a poor bunch and be told that their speech 'saved the evening', than team-up as an integral part of an overall success. But with ego inflamed in the commercial circle, they regard every speaker on the same bill as obstructions to personal success. And, should an unorthodox speaker receive a better reception than the expensively trained man, the latter will sneer at the audience for accepting such an untutored orator. But the audience remain the sole judge. If you have pleased them, you have done the job well.

The completely efficient speech-making training would be to face each student every day of the course with a completely *new* audience. He or she could make similar speeches to the day before, improved overnight as suggested, but their next set of critics would never have seen them before. Obviously this would be expensive to stage-manage, but it would be the ideal method. However, I am a great advocate of any speech-making course which aims to bring people on their feet who, in other circumstances, would remain undiscovered. So long as the natural personality is allowed to flower unfettered by too much tradition, a course can do nothing but good.

Most firms, even beyond public appearance, infuse a competitive spirit in selling. Insurance firms present prizes for best figures, points system and the like – so why retard employees' speaking styles to rigid protocols? The first speaker who has the courage to use a 'free' interpretation will obviously obtain the most interested hearing simply because he or she *is* different. Provided they put the message over lucidly without killing it with a self-opinionated approach, they will bring in the orders.

It has been whispered to me that perhaps some high-ups do not want too much competition from the up-and-comings so they have them trained on the old-fashioned lines, applying the foot-print principle of the past rather than seek to enhance originality of viewpoint. If this is so then the loss, in the long run, is the firm's itself. If you find yourself in that position, you must hold on to your personality. If you feel it is being stifled under instruction be frank with your tutors. Ask them why they are trying to change your approach. They may have a very valid reason, you may be *too* way-out and they can give a logical reason why. A true speech instructor will be grateful and will adjust his training to suit each individual under his care. However, some tutors have themselves been trained on very systemised academic lines comparatively late in life and they see no way of departing from the set formality. And perhaps they too fear competition . . . !

Certainly instructors can guide you on matters of policy, certain forms of address and technique – but they can rarely tell you about audiences. They seem to expect you to make the same speech regardless of who is out front. You, in your later wisdom, will learn assessment, you get a 'feel', an atmosphere, and will adjust your speech accordingly, much as solo variety patter acts have to do. You see – despite it being some tutors' *bête noire* – we are back to 'entertaining' again.

This has been proved conclusively to me by friends who, when giving talks on commercial subjects, have been expected to make the same speech to future staff members for their firm as they do to the Women's Institute or teenagers in their last year at school. Natural speakers adapt instinctively – but the over-trained merely parrot the same speech. Result boredom for many audiences.

One must beware of over-balancing, of being too trendy, or worse, speaking *down* to the less initiated audiences. Some speakers, in an endeavour to simplify their subject for laymen audiences, can sound, quite unconsciously, patronising. But you should get a sense of approach during your opening remarks. If you know your subject completely, you can easily adapt. But never assume they will listen to you whatever you have to say. Audiences are comprised of individuals too, remember, and your job is to mould them together in a pleased frame of mind by your speech. You may not succeed with them all, but if you carry the majority with you, you are doing your job. Never be content to please an élite minority – if there are more strangers than friends in your audience, it is the strangers who must be the first consideration.

Firms usually entrust certain talks to the man or woman directly in control of each particular aspect of their business. These may well possess the right mind to handle the facts, but are not always the best personalities to deliver them. Executives weighed down by years in the same job often sound so in their speeches. So firms might well be advised to cast around their departments for more vital speakers in matters relevant to productivity. If she has the flair to put it across, the routine annual report could be read by a competent young secretary. If she looks well, she will at least get undivided attention! Then, when questions follow, the expert can stand up and answer them – but at least some variety of speakers have been infused into the meeting. The 'one-voice' function can be deadly dull.

I suppose, 'businesswise', the chairman is expected to handle all policy speeches. It can be argued that clients expect the top man to be spokesman. But, after listening to hundreds of such speeches, I can only say that the same speaker, year after year, loses impact. When he rises, you know exactly what is in store – and that blunts interest immediately. But if a new face is before you, you sit forward. Entrusting a few of those annual speeches to others from the outer offices makes for confidence and encourages more dedication from those lower down the ladder. One of the modern handicaps of commercial progress is the apathy and lack of personal involvement by some junior staff.

So spread the speaking duties. The racy, amusing despatch clerk can be used as a compère at office parties, the clear-voiced telephonist can revitalise a dreary routine report, the accountant can hand over his monotonous set of figures to his smart, competent secretary – all providing of course they are proved to be capable in the first place. As parents should encourage their children to be unafraid of audiences, so employers should allow their younger staff to appear as their representatives in public, rather than over-use the silvered-heads of departments all the time.

But if this should be your good fortune and your firm does call on you – watch it. Many a good job has been lost at business dinners. A few drinks and the comic rises to impress with his hilarious talent – a talent his firm does not require at all in the 'hard-sell' world. Always remember that, on such occasions, to reveal a showbusiness panache could make any Big Brother watching hesitate to promote you because your heart is obviously not in your job but rather in the cabaret field.

Now I am not saying this state of affairs is a good thing ... in fact, I thank heaven I have never had to speak under these garroting conditions. But I have addressed many firms' dinners, conventions and seminars and been gently but firmly provided with material relevant to their product, their aims and objects, which I then 'forget'! My personal opinion is that the audience could well do without complete strangers brain-washing them on their own jobs, especially at social functions.

Once the Gas Council employed me at their Sales Conference to instruct their lady house-to-house demonstrators to use a modified form of showbusiness approach to their job. An enterprising Public Relations officer seemed to think I was the right

horse for that course, so I tackled it. One line I can remember :
'If any of you ladies possess a mink coat – and I'm sure working
for the Gas Council lets you run to one – do not wear it at
demonstrations in homes. Inevitably when you call you catch
the housewives in old clothes or overalls. By looking a million
dollars yourself you put them at an uncomfortable disadvantage.
So when you arrive to show them how to use their new cooker,
take off a quiet-style coat or raincoat – and put on an overall
too . . .'

It made sense and was adopted, I believe, in future briefings.
That was what I paid to do, speak relevantly of their jobs and
the image they presented to their public. But I did also manage
to raise a few laughs during the course – usually based on
'how not to do it' . . . .

I am intensely sympathetic to all of you whose jobs rely upon
speaking in public but are hidebound by certain company
'rules' which would be suicide to flaunt. We cannot turn this
trend aside . . . it is there, part of the chase for cash and status
and, if we join it, we must live – and pant – with it. Most
firms set great store by their employees' ability to say a few
words to uphold the aims of their particular industry. It is not
new – but certainly much more widely accepted than ever before. The old commercial travellers indulged in a form of it,
of course, not at boardroom or dinner table level, but across
shop counters and in pubs. Jokes by the hundred were told,
skilfully selected to impress particular customers. They knew
the hobbies of each shopkeeper, his favourite football team or
film star, and astutely sold their wares through that form of
popularity. As a little grocer once complained : 'I have tons of
salt in the back of this shop. I'll never sell that salt but the
traveller who comes here every month, oh boy, can he sell salt !'

Relevant novelty is hard to introduce in business speeches
but do your best . . . as a friend of mine once did when discussing the wide coverage of his insurance firm. Having stressed
various policies of which the average man in the street might
have no inkling, he said : 'How much do you think a dead body
is worth ?'

The room gasped. Then he went on to recount the strange
incident of a man who, when he died, had willed his body to
medical science. The body has to be transported by road over

a very long distance and the authorities wished to insure it against accident. So, how did one rate a corpse? By its almost valueless carcass content of meat, sinew, blood and water? Or by its worth for experimental purposes? And what was that? It was a vastly interesting, if macabre point, but every member of the audience certainly remembered it!

The art of persuasion must be yours when speaking on behalf of your own living. You do not have the easy sermon to the converted but to deal with wariness, suspicion and penny-pinching. If you are somewhat of a rebel, at least keep breadth of mind and a sense of humour which can sometimes cover up, quite blandly, some off-centre ideas. No employers wants anyone on their pay-roll who does not agree with company policy especially if he is liable to say so in public. Can you blame them? It may be feudal but, if you want the job, you must make concessions. So use your loaf even when you are selling someone else's.

The 'Political' Speech

'Political', I use in both senses here, the parliamentary and the more general speech which needs tact and diplomacy in community matters. In preparing speeches of this nature you must always use progressive practical material. Your speech must contain specific guidance beyond mere exhortation. A light-hearted approach can rarely be used and, if at all, only in very small doses. The humour must be apt and top standard and never descend to mockery or sarcasm. Your subject is of paramount importance and the less you complicate it with highly-personalised comments the better.

You will find when you come to write speeches of this nature, that it is all too easy to criticise conditions but devilishly difficult sometimes to offer concrete solutions to the problems. We hear too many such speeches today that stir the pot but never add one crumb of spice to improve the ingredient. Some second-rate speakers remain content to incite and provoke rather than advance any really progressive thought.

In opening such a speech it is always advisable to set your scene clearly by reiterating, if necessary, the problem so that the audience has it firmly in mind. Then you can set about your plans to improve matters. Do not dwell on anomalies too long, do not apportion blame in more than one terse sentence. Political speakers love finding culprits and spend far too long castigating opponents, time that should be used for positive, forward-looking reasoning. Usually at the end of their tirade the problem still exists and no hard solution reached. No, the entire function of a political speech should be to cure, improve or set to right a set of conditions in a positive form.

Getting a sincere political speech on paper demands that you weigh up cause *and* effect very carefully. Your audience expects practical, illustrative thought-processes from you, not honeyed words minus any sting in them. Unctious hypocrisy is the curse of political speaking as indeed it is in much general dialogue. High-minded ideals are quoted very often to cloak some very devious designs. So analyse your treatment of a political subject with the utmost care. Can you honestly admit that what you are going to say is the whole truth, half the truth or nothing like the truth? Have you a self-interest in presenting the case? Is there something more than just an ideal in it for you? Do you stand to gain if you gild the lily? If so, are you wise in taking that chance? Remember all such audiences are highly suspicious and deceiving them by committing some form of public perjury will boomerang back on you.

I have heard some snide attempts, in my time, in national and local government and these are by no means confined to Britain. Too often speakers make the mistake of appearing above reproof by virtue of their position. They assume, quite erroneously, that we are in awe of them at the outset. They open by adopting the attitude that we take it as read that they are unquestioned authority on their subject. They soon find themselves disenchanted. We want to know a valid reason why we should even consider them qualified the first place. So, in preparing such speeches, bear in mind that you can virtually assume nothing.

As a youngster I heard speeches from schoolmasters, clerics and local dignatories. Mostly they wrapped up their unsolicited criticism of us in soothing words, adopting a pretence of understanding but only seeing our scene from *their* point of view. Really to reach us they had to be our age – and desire the same girls as we did. I daresay many of them did that anyway, but their attitude was always chiding and holier than thou. So

86

naturally we never remembered anything they said.

A political speech in any of its very wide connotations needs every item of information, every strength of fact and vocabulary you can teach yourself if you are to rise above that low standard of 'old school' speakers who still bleat out epigrams. Those at the top of the parliamentary charts know the game pretty well, of course; they are past masters at stalling and hedging, but the reason they have achieved their eminence is that they are basically honest men.

If a member of parliament is your guest of honour then your audience will expect, indeed look forward to, his remarks about future prosperity – especially how it affects their personal pockets. He will be there for that express purpose. I have heard some six prime ministers and many more cabinet members and opposition at Press Club dinners in London. There they were expected to speak on current affairs. Yet I never heard one of these top-brass who did not also infuse plenty of humour in their speeches and make the evening sparkle without rancour, despite some very incisive heckling from Fleet Street newsmen in the audience. Always in good spirit, it was as entertaining as it was educative. For when a Fleet Street man heckles it is not just a mindless 'what about the workers?' chant but neat and concise point scoring, brought about by their own astute knowledge of prevailing conditions.

However, often political guests do get shouted at by some drunken diners whose prejudices, even without drink, are too strong and preclude any rational argument. They are a hell on earth because their rock-bottom minds, inflamed with alcohol, are impossible to reason with. They don't really want satisfaction – just make a nuisance of themselves. One day if you speak in this field you will meet one. You won't always hear what he slurs but always treat him courteously. Nothing silences a befuddled heckler quicker than to treat him as if he was sober. He expects hostility – so turn the other cheek. The rest of the audience know what you are about and will soon take care of him. Mark you, if they are *all* like that in the room – don't bother with them! You can't win – but you can avoid getting hurt!

Dignity is a much misapplied word. Never be on it, but never lose it. Loss of control, intolerance, impatience and stubbornness often ruin a speech which has begun well, simply because the speaker, harried off his script by interjections, will brook no criticism and has made no provision for it. If you set yourself up as an authority you must accept that someone will try and make an Aunt Sally of you. Then you must not rely on ducking and weaving out of trouble, but be in a position to throw a few scoring points back at them. If you have your facts right and the solutions you have to offer are feasible, then your speech will be worthwhile even if your remedies may seem revolutionary to some die-hards. Making a serious speech of this nature means you must know your opponents' arguments as well as your own and have them embodied into your own reasoning. And you must have absolute confidence and sincerity in yourself.

One can but generalise on 'political' speeches. The scholastic address to students or institutes is rather different. The speaker states a theory or case, even perhaps gives a practical demonstration – and his hearers can question him afterwards. This is the most civilised form of argument. But on the political platform your hearers will not wait till the end – they will often chip in with anti-argument even before you have fully propounded your case in the first place. Then you must resort to 'I am coming to that' or 'you have anticipated my next point' and so cover the question.

However, if you prepare your speech carefully you can avoid many such interruptions. One way is to commence each phase by quoting the opposition argument against it first – and then state your own antidote. This guards you against most hecklers – but not all. There are always the more moronic ones only there for the jeer.

There is a danger, of course, in such speeches, of being too erudite and talking 'over the heads' of the audience. I am sure some old-tyme speakers do this purposely. In order to overcome some tricky point of manipulation they treat their listeners to an outmoded or ultra-scientific vocabulary which befogs them, then sit down, their facts only clear to an enlightened few, usually hand-in-glove with the scheming! And if points are raised afterwards they can always prove they covered them in some rather complicated way – rather as Latin was used in medieval churches to uneducated villagers. *Argumentum ad ignorantiam!*

Avoid also being too dogmatic in your approach. Calling a

spade a spade is one thing but not a shovel. Rather than blast at them 'My opponent's idea won't work' which arouses ire at once in those who believe in it, approach the point by: 'Do my opponents see their method as solving the problem when ... ?' and so pose the question yourself without rancour.

You will need a pretty tough mechanism to enter the political arena and make speeches. Gone are the days of safe seats and touching forelocks. Nowadays you start a long way behind the old time politicians. Once at least their reputations got them off the mark before the eggs flew. But today, because of over-exposure on television, it is the fashion to denigrate celebrities so that, sometimes, the better known you are, the less chance you will have of being heard. Your opponents, too, will have little chivalry and certainly no sentiment. You must be pre-pared for a relentless battle which is both nerve-straining and exhausting – yet you must never show that on the platform. It is a world almost totally devoid of compassion.

Consideration of Speech Approach

When preparing a speech put yourself in the position of your listeners. 'If I was out there,' you say to yourself, 'what would I want to know? How would I like the subject approached?' Much depends on that subject but basically you can analyse any speech topic under the heading 'what's in it for the audi-ence?'

Many speakers, representing various industrial or commercial enterprises, give talks at schools. trying to interest the imminent school-leavers in their form of employment. The best opening I ever heard of was from a banker who wasted no time. 'If you were to join our bank you would start at X pounds a week, have a month's holiday after a year's employment and no Saturdays ...' The room buzzed with interest. Too often, in these forms of address, the mundane subject of cash is brushed aside in grandiose eulogies of team spirit and 'pulling together'. But in this highly-charged world, the kids want to know what the lolly is, how much commission they can earn, the chances of promotion and when can they afford to marry, set up home and what cash will there be to raise a family. Only then can you start expecting them to be dedicated.

That banker hit the jackpot. He went on to outline the banking system and, while I gather the headmaster deplored such mercenary approach, that speaker gained several recruits when they left school.

However, had he been speaking at a Women's Institute, his angle would have been entirely different. He would be talking to prospective customers, not possible employees. Strange to have to spell this out but, as you already know, we do find speakers who will make the same speech wherever they are. Their attitude is that an audience must accept the speech as it is ... they will not bother to adjust ... and often the results are completely negative. Do not get script-bound like this – be enterprising and use variations on your theme according to where you are speaking.

You know you must not 'attack' any audience, not even through 'nerves', nor use the bombastic style of the sergeant-major which implies 'get fell in the lot of yer'. A filibustering style is more likely to annoy an audience than the quieter delivery. So you write a speech in that vein, not giving yourself too emotive or dramatic approaches, beyond the ratio of the subject. Avoid knowing winks and guffaw-seeking 'funnies' which irritate people genuinely seeking information. Never assume that the audience will take to you right away. They want their pound of flesh and will only acclaim you if you do the job right in their sight.

Meiosis

While a certain 'contrived' modesty is allowable in speech-making do beware of 'meiosis'. A species of hyperbole representing a thing to be less than it is, meiosis is beyond mock-modesty, it is the acme of bad taste on occasions. You, in effect, play down a big event out of all proportion to its importance in another context, but include a throw-away line designed for artful self-glorification. For instance : 'I had just left Buckingham Palace after getting my knighthood when I saw this car accident...' Or – 'I was dancing with Princess Grace of Monaco when the news of the moon landings was announced...'

In each case the real subjects are a car accident and the moon ... but Pompous Percy must slip in a bit of personal social bull. Meiosis can work even more subtly than that, to becoming the form of a threat. 'We shall do our best with this new system . . . although some may lose their jobs . . . but we shall certainly try it.' In a business speech that can cause a chill. Just an 'aside', spoken as if it mattered little, but the intention is to drag in an aspect out of context or indicate the speaker's real attitude.

Meiosis is a disease also carried by 'name-droppers' who bandy the famous about in their conversation – and their speeches – but can never actually involve them in any personal anecdote. They just happened to be around. Mark you, name-dropping, if sincere, is very effective in speech-making, provided the incident is true, is entirely relevant to the subject and that the name 'dropped' plays the most important role in the development. The accusation of 'name-dropping' is often misapplied vindictively by jealous hearers to a perfectly legitimate anecdote.

'Names' are news however you may look at them and speech quotations always have an added impetus if there is a celebrity or an authority behind them. There is a tendency of 'drop-out' natures to deride and belittle anyone who has reached some sort of outstanding grade in life. Thomas Carlyle summed them up . . . 'No sadder proof can be given by a man of his own littleness than disbelief in great men.'

So, despite the pettiness that even water-tight reasons for name-dropping engenders, no one can deny that it is always a valuable experience to rub shoulders briefly with the famous in their specialised fields. Very rarely have they reached their branch of 'stardom' without talent and diligence – which perhaps their critics lack. But still beware of meiosis. No one can object to genuine pride in an achievement – but don't put your feat in your mouth in every speech!

Summary of MATERIAL AND FORMS OF SPEECHES
1. Collect material assiduously and use a filing system.
2. Do not be a 'one-speech' person – vary your material.
3. Train your memory to be alert for speech 'copy'.
4. Make sure of your facts – and get people's names right.
5. Use your local library.
6. Keep your allotted time in mind.

7. Do not be classed a copyist or plagiarist. Be creative.
8. Watch that your own 'ego' does not intrude when irrelevant to the subject.
9. Understand the difference between the *carte blanche* of a social speech and the precision of a commercial speech.
10. While keeping your personality reined within the subject, never lose it entirely, or allow it to be trained out of you.
11. The value of speaking to strange audiences rather than sympathetic pals.
12. Control when speaking for your firm.
13. The tact and diplomacy required in the political speech. Information before platitudes.
14. Control of temper with hecklers.
15. Never talk 'over the audience's head'.
16. Put yourself in the audience's place when preparing a speech.
17. Avoid 'meiosis'. 'Name-dropping' must be wholly relevant.

CHAPTER FOUR

Writing a Speech

A speech must be like a short story – have a beginning, a middle and an end. And beyond that, remember again Lord Northcliffe's terse : 'What people want is *information.*'

You know your subject, so you begin by drafting out in note form all the salient points you wish to include. Not in any specified order at this stage. Trying, at the onset, to write a speech in its final form often leads to your tailing off after a bright start simply because inspiration deserts you towards the end. So just jot down all facets to sift through for strength and relevance later on.

Your first thought, for example, is very often the climax of a speech, the highlight. This is a good peg to hang your hat on. It gives you a target, a set goal at which to aim and this aids relevancy in your development.

Before tackling the positive job of writing the speech, find out as much as you can about the function from those running it. Write to the secretary – or ring if pressed for time but better get facts in writing if possible – and, if he has not already supplied you with sufficient information, ask to be briefed on the following :

1. The 'title' of your speech. Your position on the bill. Are you opening, second, third, fourth or last?

2. Are you the principal speaker, or in support of some VI.P.?

3. Your time limit. Do not take the fact that the organisers have not given you one as an allowance to waffle on for forty minutes. They expect you to discipline yourself to a rational time, so ask what the drill is.

4. Is the event informal or black tie? This is not important to your actual speech, but it sets a seal on the type of function and also saves you the embarrassment of turning up in the wrong gear.

5. Type of audience – mixed, all-male or all-female. Also, if you can check, what sort of age-groups are involved.

6. Who your fellow speakers are? If you know any of them personally it allows you to include pleasant references. But not to settle old scores completely unconcerned with the function! If you are proposing or replying to a toast, find out the facts about your opposite number. Even if he or she is a stranger, the organisers will have some 'gen' on them to help you construct your speech. Any information, then, you can preface with: 'I understand Mr Smith is a landscape artist...' and so lead yourself into a relevant anecdote about painters... e.g. The artist who was necking with his model on his studio couch when he heard a sound of a door closing downstairs. 'My God,' he said, 'that's my wife. She mustn't see you like this. She'd suspect us at once. Get your clothes off ... !'

7. How many are likely to be present? One likes to know if a speech will be an intimate one to a few, or a big public affair to several hundred.

8. Will a microphone be used?

Go over the ground in detail as far as you can so that you are, to some extent, in the picture. You can then visualise the scene and so select and adapt any specialised material. But if some details are elusive, the safest plan is to ensure that you remain your true self certain that the lines upon which you will work allow you to speak comfortably within your compass. Never experiment on a strange audience until you have gained a lot of experience.

Your speech must be constructed as a complete 'story'. Although fragmented into sections, each must lead smoothly into the next in a fluent form. I once knew a would-be speaker who ignored Edgar Allan Poe's evocation that 'the vital requisite in all works of art is unity'. Charlie, as I shall call him, never understood style consistency. His speeches always sounded as if each paragraph was written by a different author... starting with cheery Dickensianism, he would 'ham' into Shakespeare, bump on into Elizabeth Browning, course with Chaucer, pinch from Pinter, waffle though Wodehouse, meander with Maugham and find a bit of room at the top with John Braine. Then he would end on a fanfare of 'funnies' which would have embarrassed even a porn-seller. And the awful alliteration I have used was also part of his stock in trade!

So, in one speech, Charlie the Chat would run the full gamut between the reigns of both Elizabeths, with verse, drama, puns, politics, ecology and filthy stories. One might say he tried to give value for money, but he always spoke well beyond his brief taking up at least three speakers' time. So, in trying to show his versatility, Charlie always made a complete clot of himself. On his feet he appeared a crass bore, a courier of second-hand thoughts – and yet, by a fireside, he was a most interesting and qualified chap.

Surprisingly enough not all good conversationalists are strong public speakers. They cannot sustain dialogue on their own, they need the cut and thrust of question and answer from others to stimulate their mind. As a speaker, alone on your feet, you have to press on providing your own inspiration.

Other speakers, who lack co-ordination of thought, find it difficult to discard extraneous waffle to pin-point salient thought. They will complicate an anecdote by the 'I'm a liar it was a Thursday' ploy when the day is entirely irrelevant to the plot. They become bogged down in useless detail which often leads them to forgetting the end, or worse, revealing it too early. And you know as you listen that they have not bothered to write the speech carefully.

So you prepare by writing out a speech IN FULL, jokes and all, and committing it to memory. Only then can you be sure that your delivery is crystal clear, concise – and within your time limit. That is another reason why every anecdote must be relevant to the subject. The speaker who, carried away with a desire to be funny at any price, often slips in a recently-heard gag in the middle of his speech but *has not learned with it.* The result is that it completely cuts the thread, is a *non sequita* and whether it raises a laugh or not, always leaves the speaker struggling to get back to his theme again. Never be guilty of this. If you hear a good joke on the night of your speech without time to rehearse it and blend it into your existing material, file it away for future use.

One must also, when preparing speeches, take particular care not to include embarrassing ingredients, even if they seem relevant. This can arise when you try to impress a minority in the audience with some daring remark which displeases the majority. In political fields this may be unavoidable, but in the social speech can land you in trouble. Audiences are far more sensitive than one realises. Blaspheme before drunks and they will choose that moment to see the Light. Start telling a colour bar story and in will walk a waitress from the country you are lampooning.

It is a question of keeping your sense of proportion. No man or woman in their right mind wants to be unpopular – so why court it? In a splendid speech, comedian Frankie Howerd once illustrated the differences between stories you could tell at dinners – and those you would be mad to attempt! These included jokes about Lourdes healings and being blind! His sheer professionalism raised the roof with them, but he knew his audience. He qualified these clean but sick stories as examples of inviting to be lynched. In less expert hands they could not have been countenanced even as illustrations of what not to do in a speech. Yet I bet some morons there re-told these dangerous stories as isolated 'gags' without attempting to explain them in a very special context as Frankie had done so astutely, thus giving himself a valid reason and purpose for recounting them.

Afflictions of any sort should be left out of light-hearted speeches. Stuttering stories, even the hard-of-hearing joke can upset those struggling with deaf aids in the audience. It is not being squeamish or narrow-minded – it is courtesy. So use your discretion and avoid the cheap laugh.

I once heard a lady speaker who completely stunned an audience by stressing her own ugliness. Her theme of 'always the bridesmaid, never the bride' was aimed to raise laughter but it completely misfired. We could not laugh, we were thoroughly embarrassed – and sorry for her. We felt that she was, in reality, hitting back at fate for being such a plain Jane. The audience was quite unnerved, the speaker faltered and sat down in confusion. The late Nellie Wallace could do it on music hall – but even she, dear soul that she was, found it took its toll of her for she was far from happy off stage.

So, even with stories against yourself, there must be integrity and some dignity. Be sure, when writing personal anecdotes into your scripts, that they are right for the occasion. A dash of pithy showmanship is always acceptable but 'daring' to recount a highly questionable item is asking for trouble. Horses for courses, remember.

Plotting A Speech on Paper

We already know that speeches fall into two categories, the social and the business (or political). The former is made up entirely of your personally collated material, the latter depends on already prepared hard facts and data. But into both you infuse your own ingenuity although being especially wary with the business speech.

So, with plenty of good-sized paper in front of you, consider your collected notes. Bear 'relevancy' in mind all the time as a guide line when considering whether or not each item should be included.

The Social Speech

You have been given a theme. In a book like this I cannot of course break down and analyse all the millions of subjects likely to occur in speakers' lives, but we will take as a 'social' speech model, one of the most common, the *Reply For The Guests*. From this example you will be able to adapt the format to suit other themes in the social sphere of speaking.

You have, in your rough notes, all the information you can glean about the occasion. You head the paper with the name of the event, venue, date, time allotted and the official name of your speech, in this instance: '*Reply For Guests*'.

You then write your opening line ... '*Mr Chairman, ladies and gentlemen* ...' '*My Lords, ladies and gentlemen* ...' '*Mr Mayor, lady mayoress* ...' '*Madam chairman, ladies and gentlemen* ...' etc. with 'Proposer's' name inserted second.

You will know the names of guests you will be representing if any are to be singled out in your speech. Sometimes you will be the only named one yourself so you tackle the speech with a more general approach.

Topical local events in the news might apply to the function and on the night you may hear some up to date pointers, so be prepared to include them in place of your more dated material. One cannot anticipate this, of course, but you may well have a shrewd idea of local developments so that, if nothing else, you can make your speech bang up to the minute.

Thank for hospitality with any names which need mentioning. Then include a relevant anecdote or comment, either about hospitality or one which leads from it. Perhaps you can contrast the pleasant time you are having against a poor one suffered elsewhere. Or the good food you have just enjoyed in comparison to a drab restaurant meal you had recently. Anecdotes about food are legion and, even if the anecdote is fictitious, so long as the showmanship is right, it does not matter. You may well compliment the chef – but not if the meal has been only been average which often happens these days! Never use a gag about food if the audience has just suffered a half-cold meal and poor service.

From those preliminaries you might well move on to your 'unsuitability' to propose the toast, not mock-modestly but as a laugh against yourself. Much depends upon your link with the organisers. If you know them well you can use this ploy in an amusing, personal way. But if you are a comparative stranger you have to set the scene a little more fully by explaining your 'inadequacies'. 'I sell life insurance – and you all look so healthy . . .' 'I am an optician – and I've forgotten my glasses. . .'

Then you move into the MAIN THEME – that of representing the guests and replying to the toast. Thank the proposer and make any comments arising from his or her speech. You may need to ad lib these so make notes while they are speaking. Mention any important guests by name if there are not too many of them. Otherwise your speech can sound as if you are quoting the telephone directory. If there is a V.I.P. or star guest, leave them till last on the list. Do not overstress one guest at the expense of the others unless there *is* a recognised V.I.P. And of course get your facts about them right!

You can follow the Main Theme by discussing the work or function of your host organisation, praise it sincerely – certainly never be super-critical. 'You cannot eat their salt and then pepper them,' as Sir Alan Herbert used to say. If you are a layman in their world, admit it and perhaps illustrate your paucity of knowledge by an anecdote against yourself. But do pay them the compliment of discussing their enterprise . . . without mawkish sentimentality of course.

Now you move into the final phase, the winding up. Thank the audience for their attention and try and involve them at this stage if you can. If it is a domestic audience – they usually are at such events – then a story about homelife, children, schools or even pets will apply. 'My little daughter, hearing I was going to speak at this dinner warned me not to speak with my mouth full . . .' That sort of pay-off is close to the heart of a normal, mixed audience – and even tells them you are a family man. They adore knowing *that!*

And then sit down. Do not meander on, because you will only be repeating yourself if you do. Just say 'thank you' and drop into your chair.

That, broadly, is the structure of a social speech . . . short, relevant and courteous.

The Commercial Speech

You have been asked to address a conference, meeting or even a lunch or dinner, on a business venture. It may well be one of those public-relation type speeches where you act more as an optimistic cheer-leader than add much to the audience's knowledge of the project. These pot-boiler speeches are most difficult, yet you must still try and infuse it with novelty. My advice in all such pedestrian addresses which are more ritualistic than practical, is to keep them short, very short indeed. Mostly they are courtesies of welcome to guests so be brief without, of course, being terse or off-hand.

Whatever sort of commercial speech faces you, there is usually some precedent. But, as in the social speech, you gather together the facts you must include and see just how much more vitality you can mix with them without over-playing your own personality at the expense of the subject.

To help economy in these pages, we will call the subject of your commercial speech ZENZ. So ZENZ will represent anything you, the reader, requires it to be in your particular field, a manufactured product, a scheme, insurance policy, stocks, shares, agreement, contract, programme, advertising campaign, publicity stunt – you name anything in your own trade palaver and ZENZ will be it!

99

So – you have to speak on ZENZ.

Again, as with the social speech, you jot down details of venue, date, etc., although you may not have been given an allotted time. If it has been left to your discretion, be as brief as possible. Obscure the vital story of ZENZ with a lot of personal asides and you may well fail to make the correct impact.

Make sure you have all the names of those involved, the chairman, and others on the speaking bill, dividing those who will support you and those (if any) who will oppose you.

Check all the 'for' and 'against' arguments, especially arming yourself with the latter. Do as much homework as you can to avoid being stumped by an awkward question when you are on your feet. But if you become involved in industrial espionage to get your facts, don't blame me! However if ZENZ is a delicate hush-hush subject you will not be entrusted to speak on it until you are experienced enough to know exactly the right tactics to employ.

Study all the facts of ZENZ at your command closely for relevant, additional material which illustrates its value. You may have access to anecdotes (not necessarily funny but useable as shrewd examples). Perhaps you can rustle up *Financial Times* quotes, trade press, prices, costs, economics, to indicate its value to the community or commercial fields. Prepare to refute certain foreseeable criticism, backing your arguments with logic, not prejudice.

You will be persuading your audience to accept ZENZ in some particular aspect. ZENZ is being bought or sold. Never avoid that stark issue by high-toned moralising or phoney sentimentalism. If ZENZ is on the market, profit for its creators cannot be brushed aside. Putting forward the argument that ZENZ will benefit mankind, that you are doing the community a service by introducing it, is for the guillables of television comcercials only. Yet a lot of old die-hards do practice this hypocrisy still, hoping the audience will ignore profit motive. None of them will. Their attitude is 'what's in ZENZ for me?', so always speak candidly.

Selling is a technique much reliant upon personality, so do not entirely lose your identity in a long, unrelieved, statistical drone. If the audience has confidence in the speaker, they will have confidence in his wares. But if he should over-sell himself, then the reaction can be to treat the product with scepticism too. 'What's he trying to hide with all this blather about himself?' they think. And yet waffle, 'um' and 'er' and be hesitant, then you may well discredit ZENZ when it is a perfectly laudible enterprise.

Wind-up with a brief recapitulation of the facts, but do not allow the fact that the audience has behaved impeccably throughout snare you into feeling you must prolong your speech. Many a business speaker ruins a perfectly good commercial discourse by going off at tangents when summing up. Inevitably he takes longer to round-off his subject than he did to discuss the main theme. Time allocations may not be rigid in this form of speaking – but discipline yourself for the sake of your reputation. You cannot leave an audience actually wanting more in this field – if they are truly interested they should know all about ZENZ at the end of your talk – but present it succinctly. Do not wear out its welcome.

Right, there are the rough outlines for two kinds of speeches, the social and the commercial. Now you have to sort through the accumulated data and write out the speech in full.

The Final Speech on Paper

You do not have to be an author to write a good speech. If you can write a competent letter you will be probably much better. Really imaginative writers are apt to over-phrase a speech, forgetting that what looks well in print can sound ponderous or poetic when spoken in public, especially on commonplace subjects. So keep your language simple.

When writing you must attune your mind to the function. Is it basically a serious or light-hearted occasion? There are varying shades of demeanour in speech-making as contrasting as a court martial to an all-male night at the football club, a flower arranging society to Women's Lib. Somewhere among the hundreds of degrees of suitable approaches will be the one best suited for you to present.

That is the fascination of public speaking. You will, as you become established, find yourself asked to speak at some surprising events. Men used to stag parties are suddenly facing all-female audiences. Ladies used to women's social club functions unexpectedly have an audience of hawk-eyed businessmen. So they have to change their approaches to some degree, or fail.

Writing a speech is like editing a magazine. You have to please your overall circulation of different readers in the way they all expect to be entertained or educated. They know the *policy* of the magazine and you, as editor, have to ring the subtle changes on it – but always keeping *within* it. Speech writing is a splendid exercise and cannot be dashed off like a scribbled message on a phone pad.

You know your first line, be it 'Mr Chairman' or just 'comrades'. But do give an introduction. I know some students who despise it, who will bark straight into their theme without preliminaries, but this often means their early points are lost in the general buzz which usually heralds a speech. If your invitation to rise and speak has been a hasty one, say at a seminar rather than formally from a toastmaster or chairman, with merely a pointed finger to indicate you can say your piece, then you are wise to address the meeting with a definite opening, introductory line. However unimportant it may be to your theme, it does ensure you get silence. 'Ladies and gentlemen . . .' then pause, as the room settles to listen . . . 'I would like to make this point' (or words to that effect) . . . and only then take up your argument. Rush into a speech and you can throw away a vital piece of evidence. You have to start by taking not so much command as control over the audience.

So in writing your speech you will find that you have four distinct phases :
1. Introduction
2. Reason for making speech
3. Main Theme – your 'big sell'
4. Wind-up and close.

From your notes you sort out the correct running order of each phase, making each one complementary to the next and rising to a pleasing climax, rather than start strongly and then fade away.

Bridging Links

The fault in amateur speakers in their early days is very often lack of good 'bridging links'. Take this example :

You have been talking about shopping problems and you use

the following anecdote: '*A lady I know of suddenly burst into tears in the local supermarket. The manager consoled her and asked what the trouble was. 'My telly has broken down,' she sobbed 'and now I can't see the commercials I don't know what to buy!'*'

Then you continue:

'*Television plays such an influential part in our lives. We can see both comedians and cabinet ministers in our own living-rooms – and sometimes cannot tell the difference. But even the political scene is changing. The Prime Minister has said...*' and so on.

Each paragraph is the bridging link, taking you from 'shopping' to 'the Prime Minister', via 'television'. While the gags may be corny the effect is smooth. You don't hop from the supermarket, to television, to the P.M. in three unrelated phases. They are all linked – or bridged – so that the speech moves forward fluently, each succeeding idea related to the last by reference so that you have a continuous, relevant story.

If bridging links are omitted when your write the speech, you will end up with a very jerky effort indeed. Often a speaker will use the 'that reminds me' ploy which is very rarely a true statement of fact. And can lead to gaffes such as one made by a speaker who, having just paid a fulsome tribute to the lady chairman, suddenly said: 'Which reminds me there was this Soho call girl...'

There are more stumours and unconscious insults caused by poor bridging links than in other structures of a speech. Isolated, both sections of a speech can be harmless – but if badly linked, can cause offence. So train yourself in speech writing to merge each change of aspect, and make one lead to the other.

Other examples spring to mind. If you are talking about town planning, and want to move on to street lighting ... you might link with '*and with town planning and new homes, the streets must be lit at night...*' Quite simply you ease into the change of aspect through '*new homes*'.

When toasting guests at a dinner you can link each guest by linking one name with the next; '*We are pleased to see Mr Smith from Wimbledon here tonight and, from further afield, is Mr Jones from Birmingham.*' The insertion of '*further afield*' saves it from sounding too much like a catalogue. One wants to be brief about these matters but never abrupt.

You do not need a high literary IQ to write bridging passages. It is just common sense and, once established in the mind, makes speech writing so much easier.

Speakers are inclined to put down their main points and hope for bridging link inspiration on the night. But they must be learned as part of the main speech in the first place.

If you find you have to drastically change course – then say so. Lines like *'which bring me to my second point'* or *'changing the subject completely'* are perfectly acceptable as they clarify to the audience your new tack and so prepare them for an entirely new aspect. Speeches at functions sometimes have to include information to members beyond the theme of the night. Chairmen in particular have to dodge from pillar to post with announcements and isolated information. So be emphatic about it, do not slur into changes of aspect after a funny story as if it was an addendum to it – but pause and prepare them by a brief introductory remark ....*'while I am on my feet the secretary has asked me to tell you that the annual meeting ...'* and so on. Don't begin on *'the annual meeting'* or someone may well miss the news!

Time Allowance

You will know what length in minutes you have been allotted for your speech. So, when the script is written in full, you must adapt it to suit your brief. So we can break down a speech, say, of ten minutes into the following sections:

1. Introduction.	$\frac{1}{2}$ min.
2. Reasons for presence, replies to points raised	$2\frac{1}{2}$
3. Main Theme including anecdotes	$6\frac{1}{2}$
4. Thanks and pay-off	$\frac{1}{2}$
	10 mins.

That format can be adjusted for longer – or even shorter – speeches. When imparting information the less you actually say, the more your audience will remember. So you prune your speech according to your alloted time.

The tendency is always to write too much. If a function is purely social then cut the duller portions. I know it is difficult to assess which, if any, of your deathless prose is dull, but pare it down you must. Believe me, the audience will not share your view that every word is a gem if you go on too long. Ten minutes may seem all too short a time for you to register your glowing personality – but it is an eternity to an audience if you bore them. There is an old speaking maxim which says 'if you haven't struck oil in two minutes, stop boring.'

You can speak about 120 to 140 words to the minute so use a stop-watch or the second-hand of your wrist watch and time yourself. Some of us speak faster than others, but if you aim at around 130 words per minute you should end up with a natural speed for your own individual delivery.

Vary the lengths of the sentences you write for yourself, remembering what we discussed earlier about space to breathe. Divide them contrastingly, some short, some in two, some in three parts using the conjunctions 'and', 'but' etc. Certainly never lumber yourself with very long sentences. I prefer one conjunction per sentence but also I use the pause.

Do not of course make them *all* short conjunctionless sentences! I have heard a stunted sentence speech by a newcomer. It sounded like series of tommy-gun bursts – and it certainly mowed the audience down, killing them stone dead! No, let the speech flow evenly but unhurriedly.

Speech Examples – Use of Contrast

It is not possible in any one book to quote examples of every type of speech you may deliver in a lifetime but continuing the study we made of that evergreen social standby speech, in 'Replying for the Guests' we have probably come up with something like this.

'Mr Chairman, ladies and gentlemen. It is a great honour for me to be replying to this toast ... but also somewhat bewildering. I must, among all the guests present, be the least qualified. Mr Green has paid us wonderful tributes which I am sure my fellow-guests can all live up to – but I am certain I can't fill the bill. For instance, my job as ...'

Then move into an anecdote which reveals your 'unsuitability', e.g. if it is a tennis club, your game is golf; if it is an insurance dinner, you are an architect, and so on. This allows to effect that vital ingredient which lifts a speech beyond the cut-and-dried traditional format – Contrast.

Not every speech allows you to make use of much contrast. Ritualistic courtesies, formal orations, simple speeches of thanks – contrast is not expected in them and, if inserted, could cause a jarring note by going off the accepted beaten track. Contrast forced into the conventional canons of speech-making can upset accepted custom. Her Majesty the Queen when declaring Parliament open does not begin 'A funny thing happened to my husband and me on our way to the House . . .'

But in un-strait-jacketed speech-subjects contrast is the best way to infuse novelty. You don't have to make yourself out to be a complete mug if your line of country is different from your audience's . . . you just view the subject from a different angle.

'Being completely new to your field, I can only express my admiration for what you do . . .'

Then you can 'bridge' into a topical reference, local conditions or something particular to the society or audience you are addressing, with all your facts checked of course. If you insert a relevant anecdote, do be sure it is one not likely to be so well-known to the room as a hoary old historic joke, but something you yourself have adopted as an illustration from your collected material.

Say, for example, your host club is famous for charity fundraising; after you mention it glowingly, you can use Contrast, say with a story about mean or penny-pinching people. Your bridging link might work like this . . .

. . . your generous work and time given so unsparingly in a good cause. Unlike the married couple who won half a million on the football pools. The wife was very worried. 'What,' she asked her husband, 'shall we do about the begging letters?' He replied: 'Send them out as usual.'

This sort of contrasting showmanship makes the room feel expansive. And if you tell the gag properly they will be amused. You have involved *them* in the joke – not isolated it an irrelevant 'funny'.

This leads quite effectively into your winding up passages. You wish them good luck in the future. Finally thank all concerned *on behalf of all the guests,* not personally, as your speech must not lose sight of your brief. If the hospitality has been outstanding and the food good, mention it . . . e.g. (bridging link) *'a great change from the canteen meals to which I am used. I just could not get over the fact that tonight my knife and fork were not chained to the table . . .'*

That sort of absurdity always proves popular at light-hearted affairs, especially at firm's dinners where canteens are all too familiar to the audience.

Then you thank again the proposer of the toast and sit down.

For the commercial or political speech, the format is different. Humour and whimsicalities must not predominate although, if used subtly, can infuse a certain contrast in your words. But you must be very diplomatic in the use of humour. It must be one hundred per cent relevant or it will be obvious to the audience that you are merely trying to show off. And if it does sound contrived you can lessen both your own image and the impact of your subject. Humour can be a dangerous double-edged weapon, especially if you take the micky out of your job in front of those paying you to do it!

But, if your subject contains 'do's' and 'don'ts' in advice form, humour might be used in examples of how NOT to do the job, of getting fouled up by not following correct procedure. A laugh at the expense of some anonymous chump will press the information far deeper into a listener's mind than merely a brief warning without any actual illustration of the dangers involved.

In the commercial or political speech you open in the same way, addressing the chairman and room in general – but courtesies are kept to a minimum. Get right to the crux of the matter in hand in your second sentence . . . *'Mr chairman, ladies and gentlemen, ZENZ is . . .'* and on you go, imparting information, advice, suggestions, recommendations with complete regard for salesmanship in accordance with your brief.

But do not indulge in large blocks of weighty, unrelieved data, break up items with anticipated queries in the audience's mind. *'What has ZENZ to offer the housewife/wool merchants/ building trade . . . ?* You effect your contrast by self-imposed questions to placate any doubts, reservations or misapprehensions you feel the audience may have. You will always know whether or not your audience is selective and how much they already know about ZENZ. There is no need for me to emphasise the dangers of over-enthusiasm causing over-selling. Make ZENZ out as invincible and someone may spend the rest of your speech concentrating upon loopholes in your early arguments and so ignore your subsequent words. And, at question time, may well ask something they have missed. Nothing shows up a speaker's inefficiency more than receiving questions at the end that he has actually covered in his speech.

Only you can be the judge of whether you want questions during your speech or when you have finished it. Much depends on your subject. If a complicated one, it might be a good notion to invite questions, phase by phase. But if you adopt this method, you must also be a strong chairman, otherwise you run the risk of a plethora of queries on one particular aspect so bogging you down that others have to be glossed over, later on, against the clock.

Much better to complete your talk on ZENZ uninterrupted with the members of the audience taking notes, and then invite questions.

In political speeches, it is rare that this orderly format can be put into practice. Questions are shot at you, both sensibly and moronically, throughout the whole speech. Attenders of political meetings are there to find out what's in it for them. And what may suit the national interest may not suit some individual's purse. As the Secretary of the United Nations once said: 'The gulf between aspiration and reality will always exist.' One man's idea of human rights often destroys another's. That is why, in political speaking outside a one-party meeting, you will rarely, if ever, please the audience as a whole. There will always be some diffused characters wanting to grind their particular axe. And, in this increasingly belligerent world, axe is the operative word.

So, in the political field, you cannot expect as much good order or courtesy as in the social or business speech. As you face that glowering, frowning audience, always bear in mind that the National Anthem they will all rise to is 'God save OUR gracious thing'.

I wish you joy and admire your pluck. A warm flannel removes egg stains.

Getting Off the Mark
It is vital to open a speech convincingly. Start hesitantly, seemingly unsure of yourself, and it is hard to effect a really vital

recovery. It is a tense moment, I agree, but don't wreck your chances by charging off at the speed of light, as I mentioned before, and losing your opening lines in applause or the general background clatter of a settling room.

Study any opening you write very carefully. Not only from your point of view but the audience's as well. Is there too much preamble? Or will they hitch on to your motive immediately?

You must open relevantly to your speech theme. Never make the mistake of some bumbling tangent, sideline or even joke entirely divorced from your subject. If you are going to amuse them they will know soon enough. Would-be comics often try and 'give themselves an "entrance" ' as the saying goes. The best humorists let their style creep up on an audience, beginning sometimes perfectly seriously. The dawning realisation that the speaker is entertaining is part of the joy of hearing him.

So never over-complicate a speech opening. It is the frontispiece of your story while the audience is still assessing you visually. You may have to set your scene more warmly after the toastmaster's cold impartial announcement to invoke an atmosphere of enthusiasm. Certainly do not indulge in 'shock' openings designed to create a 'boat-rocking' reaction. Only a very experienced speaker can, say, on proposing a toast to 'the Ladies', open with: 'I hate women!' It has been done by clever cynics who actually use it brilliantly as a compliment to the fair sex, contrasting their own inability to cope with their sheer charm and talent. It is nothing more than a leg-pull, but don't chance your inexperienced arm with such a tactic in the early days. One needs a certain acting ability to hoodwink an audience with such an opening. It could sound genuine and cause offence if you cannot sustain it. Gimmick openings, even when we have been at the speaking game some time, can have a way of going sour on us.

Over-effusive sentimental openings are embarrassing to audiences especially if you are a stranger to them. We are back to that dangerous assumption that we feel the audience have assessed us already as the awfully good companion to the world at large. Audiences rarely take that view of a stranger; they want proof before they will grant you any licence to be a dear old pal.

Much depends on whether your introduction is from the toastmaster or the chair. The former will be short, to the point, but the latter may rabbit on a bit about your 'expertise', your qualifications for the speech. Strictly speaking, a chairman should ask how you would like to be announced. If there *is* a toastmaster tell him just what you like said about you so that his introduction can form a 'bridging link' to lead smoothly into your opening remarks.

In my case, having two professional occupations, I usually appear at functions as either a writer or an actor – very rarely as both. So, according to the occasion, I ask that I am introduced in the one most suited. If referred to as an actor I can then open with ... 'You may have seen me on television – if you were quick ...' This sometimes raises a chuckle because the audience then realise I do not regard myself as a star performer and I can then go on to tell them of the trials and tribulations of a mere support player.

However, if I am there in my writing capacity, I usually begin 'Recently in a Brighton junk shop I picked up a tattered copy of my first novel, marked two pence. 'Useful book that,' said the stall-holder. 'Useful?' I asked puzzled. 'Yes, it propped up the leg of my wife's sewing machine for years ...'

The story is true and, among people interested in writing, it gets a smile. If you can work on that principle, painting a pertinent picture at the onset, it certainly gets you off the mark. Remember *'There is a willow grows aslant the brook ...'* in its uncomplicated beauty. Once an audience is busy forming mind pictures you have their fascinated attention, the room unified in concentration, everyone with their particular version appearing in their skull cinema.

I remember a veteran beginning his speech about motor roads, something on these lines: *'As a schoolboy I trailed reluctantly up that road. I disliked the curves, the corkscrew twists. A straight road would have saved me endless bad marks for being late. Today that road is straight – and now school children are at risk of being maimed or killed by speeding traffic. The pace of so-called progress can halt forever the progress of many unlucky children. How fortunate I was that the road twisted when I was young ...'*

Emotive perhaps, but effective in its context. That type of

comparison, the illustrative opening, can be applied to amusing as well as serious subjects, a personal involvement from the speaker which encompasses the community at large.

If your speech is intended to amuse, then you can open with a relevant quip. Examples spring to mind from over the years. Lord Chief Justice Goddard frowning round a packed room and beginning: 'Some of you look very familiar – haven't I sentenced one or two of you?' Comedian Arthur Askey at a military dinner, up-ending the microphone to the floor, saying; 'I must test this place for mines first.' The mature lady replying for the guests, having been announced as 'Miss', opening with: 'I may be a spinster but I'm not one of the miserable ones . . .'

Playing yourself down, putting a low-sighted perspective on your life automatically puts an audience on your side. Only if you are an acknowledged expert in your field and the speech is a serious one, should you unashamedly rule the roost. But we, the average folk with no claims to fame, are safer if we imply life is a great leveller. All audiences have suffered like experiences and can chuckle with you. A sure laugh is dignity brought down – the fall that follows even pardonable pride.

The Main Body of the Speech

A speech must sustain interest throughout. It is useless getting off to a bright, bonanza start and then slipping down the scale like the productivity graph of a bad year. Your speech should be designed in an ascending scale so that you end on a climax. Once you lower the standard of material or drop the tempo, so, too, will the audience droop and, however bright your conclusion, you will never recapture them. Avoid making your speech like a hammock, safely topped and tailed but sagging in the middle. That is why the over-long speech fails. One is reminded of Sir William Harcourt's advice to young speakers: 'Think of your first sentence, then your last – and bring them as close together as possible.'

You have to maintain 'salesmanship'. The audience will regard your speech as a form of 'product'. Is there anything in it for them? Will it stimulate their thinking? Or their sense of humour? There are snob audiences of course. Oh, yes. If a public figure is speaking they will chuckle knowingly at his bon mots, and 'hear-hear' all over the room just to get into the act and bask in his reflected glory. But, if 'unknown', we have a bigger task on our hands than a 'name' speaker. We can only succeed by knowing our subject intimately and deliver our speeches in an entertaining manner.

So the main body of our speech must be constructed on sticking to the point. Its strength will lie in making our bridging links apposite, and maintaining an interesting flow of information. The audience do not want to be obviously taught; they want to absorb material which they can, as they do so often, pass off later as their own knowledge, as they do that which they once learned at school.

I repeat – stick to the point. Remember amid a lot of thread-bare cliches which could be erased from public speaking, one remains valid: 'There's a time and place for everything.' Again I stress if your job is to propose the guests' health do not seize on that opportunity to crack the whip against the local council just because the mayor is in the chair. To use a social speech for vote-catching of any sort is cheap and nasty – and yet some speakers are still incredibly naïve or pompously stupid in this context.

Once I heard a devastating reply to one such speaker: 'Mr Brown, in proposing the health of our club captain has somehow involved the Archbishop of Canterbury who is not here, a local traffic problem of juggernaut lorries which do not seem to be passing through this room tonight and has also advocated free contraceptives at the Health Centre ... perhaps if his parents had such an advantage he would not have been here himself!'

Tough talk – but that tub-thumper asked for it. Your speech must suit the occasion, the platform be correct for every view you air.

In the main body of a speech beware of dwelling too long on mere peripheral aspects of your main theme. For example, if you addressing aspiring footballers, they do not want to be regaled about the past triumphs of your own club all the time. Certainly when you won the Cup is important to them, but they want to know how they can get into the big league rather than the game's history. If you are talking about painting as a hobby, your audience do not want Rembrandt's life-story, although perhaps one anecdote from it will prove a point in art itself. An M.P. will not impress his constituents with a long discourse on his personal memories of Churchill – but certainly one vital reference to him might be extremely valid.

I remember, too, a titled owner of a stately home give, as an after-dinner speech, what must have been a version of the conducted tour he made when being followed round his mansion by florin-paying tourists. It was deadly dull. We could not see the ceilings, pictures or silverware he described. It would have been far more to the point if he had made a comparison between the running of a stately-home by his ancestors and the work entailed in its upkeep today. But, as he presented it, it was like a television commentary – without picture. My quiet guess is that that it was the only speech he knew anyway!

Too many speakers confuse lectures with speeches – of which more anon. But do ensure that you do not over-use *associated* themes with your main subject. They may seem relevant at first glance, but with analysis you will find they are only brushing the extremities and are not the heart of the matter.

The Emotive Appeal

'As I stand here, I feel that I must call you "friends". I see your happy, smiling faces around me. I am deeply moved. This moment brings the realisation of the true wealth of friends. No man is poor if he has friends, friends who will stand by him, through thick and thin...in my treasure chest of memories there dwells...'

YUK! A thick-hide making a thin speech. That to some rhetorical old hams is a speech. And sub-edit what that arch humbug has said it boils down to 'Thanks for your hospitality'. That same flowery-phraser is also always coy when referring to women guests – even to calling his own spouse 'my lady wife' as if he has a few of the other kinds at home as well!

Yet, study this next speech, from a club secretary to whom a gift has just been presented.

'Mr Chairman, ladies and gentlemen,

I deeply appreciate the honour you have accorded me to-night. What I have done for the club has not, I assure you, been any sacrifice on my part. I was glad of the opportunity to put back a little effort into a club which has brought me so much personal pleasure over the years. The friends I have made, the good times I have had and the pride you have all taken in the club's well-being, have acted as a spur to my own role in running its affairs. That I could share my enthusiasm with you in some tangible way was as much my pride as my duty. I enjoyed every minute of it and I shall treasure this kind gift as a memory of some wonderful days. Thank you very much indeed.'

That short, to-the-point speech cannot fail. Compare it with the earlier 'sob story'. Both say much the same thing yet the second is devoid of sloppy sentimentality. Dignity has been maintained without histrionics or attempts at tear-jerking. And you can see just how out of place and irrelevant a joke would be if included under these circumstances. A speech like the latter one is ideal if, for example, at such a club function, dancing is to follow the speakers and everyone is rearing to gyrate . . . for that speech, with all its apposite content, takes only around 50 seconds!

Getting Out of Your Depth
In commercial speaking we should rarely be in trouble simply because we are invited as already accepted experts in our subject. But at social functions we might find ourselves standing up when the theme of the evening is not quite our cup of tea. Then, in an endeavour to please entirely *within* the theme, minus experienced sea-legs we might go overboard and land on the rocks.

Take golf as an example. If you don't play yourself, don't tell golf stories. You may search joke books diligently but the ones you find are bound to be chestnuts to the assembled devotees. A *new* golf story is a rare gem indeed and unlikely to come the way of anyone untutored in the game. I have heard many well-intentioned speakers trotting out all the whiskery old golf gags and being stranded completely in the 'rough' as no one laughed.

So, if the central theme is not your scene, tell them at the onset – and then provide *contrast*. Being a light-hearted occasion you can break the relevancy rule simply because you have been asked to speak purely to entertain and it is in the interest of the audience that you put yourself on familiar ground. So you can, in all fairness, say : *'Ladies and gentlemen, as you know golf, so*

I know gardening/electronics/plastics/hockey/what-have-you...' If you are bright and amusing *within* your own orbit and do not blind them with its science, you will give your hearers a welcome change from the other speakers tied to the expertise of the theme. But do make your discourse amusing – never try to educate them in a serious vein on such nights. They'll stymie you if you do.

As one often faced with this dilemma I usually wriggle out of it by using association of ideas. Golf is full of rabbits whose ambition is to be Open Champion. So one can use that same Walter Mitty outlook to switch it to walk-on actors wanting to play Hamlet, or public park footballers dreaming of appearing in the World Cup. Provided the material is aimed to amuse it can easily provide the best *contrast* in the whole night's speaking.

Closing a Speech

The inexperienced speaker inevitably ends too abruptly. I am all for brevity but not slamming on the brakes. *'Well,'* gasps the nervous one, *that's all I have to say,'* and sits down. It is no compliment to the audience to be so summarily dismissed! If the speech is properly prepared you will end on the brief courtesies and thanks ... *'well, my time is up – save to thank you all for your attention ...'* Just a few words added – but a whale of a difference in good manners.

Or there is the long-distance speaker who says: *'And finally ...'* (at which the room stirs in relief) – and yet takes another 23 minutes to sum up. His *'in conclusion'* so often takes up three-quarters of his already over-run speech – including injury time!

So, when preparing a speech on paper make sure you do not waffle on with newly inspired thoughts, but stick to your intention to wind-up in two brief sentences. Some will tell you that to begin your last sentence with 'finally' on 'in conclusion' is the sign of the amateur. It only becomes that, frankly, if having made that statement, you go on for another ten minutes. There is no harm in signifying your intention to round off your speech but do so, deftly and quickly. *'I cannot sit down without thanking your society for being such splendid hosts ...'* a courteous formality and takes one line of dialogue. And, as the cabaret comedians put it, 'it gets you off'.

Another form of amusing pay-off is one that destroys all that you have said, the surprise ending, which illustrates a completely contrary angle. For example, Alan Paul, the late-lamented BBC musician, once took a taxi from Broadcasting House. The taxi-driver slid back his window and asked Alan what he did on the radio.

'I write music,' he said flattered.

'I should have thought,' said the driver contemptuously, 'there was quite enough of that about already.'

After a brilliant musical discourse Alan often rounded it off with that squelch – and it never failed to get a big laugh. Finish on the 'shattering' of your own illusions and you will sit down to big applause.

But by far the best note to close any speech is OPTIMISM. End on a cheerful note even if the speech has been serious. Some speakers, having raised laughter, do sometimes close on a semi-serious note, but they should be brief about it – not herald it with *'to be serious for a moment'* – just ease into it. *'Ladies and gentlemen, just before I sit down I would like to pay tribute to . . .'* That is a sufficient bridging link to get you into your short closing sentences. And if you have had the audience's undivided attention throughout, they will slip into the same mood-gear as yourself without any jogging from you.

In closing a speech never forget to thank people if it is your duty so to do. Too many times have I heard important helpers omitted. I have seen club secretaries and treasurers completely disregarded when they have organised the whole evening, laid on the meal, arranged the speakers and cabaret and sent out the invitations single-handed. Everyone else is thanked from the chair, including the chef and hotel manager who, after all, are being paid to do their jobs. The chairman will pay effusive tributes to the girl singer but completely ignore her hard-working pianist. While it is always a pleasant courtesy to thank even professionals at a function, the kind people who have genuinely given their services must top the appreciation bill. Many a willing but outspoken club worker has resigned through being left out of a speech of thanks.

But if you are a 'guest' speaker do not step out of your brief and thank people with whom you are not concerned. You are liable to take words out of the chairman's mouth and this makes for repetition. Well-meaning guests, flushed with a speaking success, often make this mistake when they are head-over-heels in love with a responsive audience. They just have to capitalise on every aspect on the function to stay on their feet. It is bad technique and eats up valuable speaking time – so, as a guest, pay tribute only to those directly concerned with your own speech.

The Final Script
So bearing in mind the hazards to avoid, the courtesies to be included and the theme of the speech, we set it down on paper. Not on the backs of envelopes or corners of shopping lists but on quarto, A.4 or foolscap, the handwriting or typing widely spaced so that you can insert corrections and after-thoughts.

Plot so that the big moments are balanced throughout the speech, not altogether in a clutch which makes the rest of the speech dull by comparison. Build up the speech in ever-increasing interest rather than hit the jack-pot too early. But, if your best lines have to come earlier than you expect – stop there. Better a short speech of real worth than one spoiled by being dragged out after the highlight has been reached. Never feel obliged to speak the full ten minutes if you find you can say all you want in seven. No organiser will blame you for that – indeed most likely welcome it. Many a good speech has been wrecked by inapposite jokes tagged on at the end just to fill in time. But my bet is that you will have included more material than you can use in the time allowed.

So cut down fearlessly and save the unused material for another speech. Pay particular attention to your bridging links, for they are both cues to remind you of what comes next – and the fluency of your speech. You will redraft the speech several times, especially as you get the 'feel' of it. Inspiration will increase as you become familiar with the content; you will alter and improve.

But beware of being over-ambitious. Very often first thoughts are best. The original concept is often the most imaginative, created when the idea of the speech is fresh, and thus more likely to retain the necessary simplicity. At the onset your mind is not complicated by visualising the actual act of speaking. In getting to know the speech more thoroughly, you can over-reach yourself in assessment of ability and through the growing confidence of rehearsal get out of your depth by exhibitionism. Then nerves on the night will do the rest and the venture go off disappointingly for you.

So in writing your early speeches, make things easy for yourself by keeping well within your limitations of vocabulary and voice-power.

Professionally-written Speeches

These are rarely available for the beginner, but certain busy tycoons do have speeches written for them by professionals. Indeed one or two comedians run speech-writing services – and I have written a few myself. But there are snags. So often you only hear the client on the phone and you have little notion of his true personality. And inevitably a man who uses a professional script writer changes personality himself when he rises to his feet – you can never truly judge his ability unless you have already heard him in public first. Thus, you may well give him something his character is completely devoid of handling. Usually you aim to keep the speech very straight-forward and he will 'pretty' it up himself with a few of his own choice phrases – the net result being of course a hotch-potch of clashing styles.

I readily understand pressurised businessmen needing a speech-writer when harassed by time. I have known company directors rely on their secretaries for a quick speech. Many a Fleet Street editor relies on a 'sub' to knock something up. The result usually sounds what it is, the scrapings of a hasty visit to the reference library. They may have to find out details of some Guest of Honour but can only, against the clock, list his achievements flatly, unable to embue it with the man's character. I realise it is difficult to speak of anyone in public if you have never met them before. But too many speakers try and twist the personalities of their guests to be someone they are not – just to fit into their idea of a speech. So guests find themselves on the receiving end of the wrong speaker, the serious professor in the hands of a sexy joke teller and the dishy television actress being analysed technologically by the scientist.

However, the professional writer can help experienced speakers. Usually all they want is three or four jokes about certain subjects they have to cover in an unexpected speech. And, sometimes, don't want to pay for them when they get them! They time them badly, tell them hesitantly and when they fall flat, condemn the writer, not their own inability to handle humour. Writing speeches for others is a dog's life. The writer is always blamed – even when the speaker tries to deliver the speech half-paralysed with drink!

Summary of WRITING A SPEECH

1. Give your speech a beginning, middle and end.
2. Give full time to it, not work on it at odd moments between other leisure activities.
3. Inform rather than teach.
4. Keep simple, remembering that one effective word per sentence is better than over-elaboration.
5. Use punctuation judiciously and take into account breath pauses.
6. Do not confuse candour with insult. Weigh up carefully any controversial statements you intend to use. Too many speakers are clever without being wise.
7. Be your own critic. Put yourself in your audience. 'Live and let live.'
8. Be yourself.
9. Write in accordance with your time limit – and stick to it.
10. Check your facts – and do not forget to thank people.
11. Use Contrast as an ingredient for your speeches.

CHAPTER FIVE

Learning a Speech and Using Notes

In early speaking days most of us will prefer to learn a speech by heart. For the record, why 'by heart' and not 'by memory'? Well, the term arose from the correct English translation of 'apprendre par coeur', but the French has mis-translated the Latin 'apprehendre per chorum', which defined the repetition system of learning when pupils chanted 'in chorus' possibly without very much 'heart'! The English translated Perrault's 'Cinderella', badly, too, mis-reading 'vair' for 'verre' and gave her a glass instead of a fur slipper! So, like that impossible footwear, 'learning by heart' became lore.

But parrot-fashion speaking can endanger its spontaneity, make it stilted and lack light and shade in delivery. The speaker is apt to concentrate too heavily upon remembering the words rather than infuse them with personality. He knows what to say but is short on *how* to say it. Word-perfect beginners, for example, mostly forget to smile or even change their facial expression at all.

Of course with a business speech demanding pin-pointed accuracy, you cannot risk breaking down or waffling as if trying to seek inspiration from the ceiling. However, in the beginning you are not likely to be entrusted with such a speech and so you can gradually equip yourself to handle one after you have been through a series of social occasions which will condition you to face audiences.

If you should possess that useful gift, a photographic memory, be careful to maintain rhythm and style. Many amateur actors blessed with super-retentive minds are very often wooden in movement and delivery. In the learning of the lines they do not inherit the character; the words are learned as mere words, not as the dialogue of a thinking person. So it is with speechmaking. Your can so learn and deliver a speech, giving it a flat, monotonous presentation that your friends will tell you it doesn't sound like you at all. I have seen such speakers, their eyes fixed dead ahead on the opposite wall, reeling off their speech like a vegetable catalogue. No zip, no zing, no showmanship. When this stoniness is pointed out to them, the next time they are on their feet they will try to rectify inamination with threshing, gymnastic gestures, so becoming oratorical hams of the worst order.

Certainly knowing the words off pat makes you feel safer, but beware of, in effect, sounding every comma and full stop as well. You must be sufficiently relaxed to give the lines an 'ad lib' impression. One does need a little stagecraft, of course, but the best insurance for presenting yourself with repose and style is knowing your subject so well that it appears part of your personality to talk about it.

The best practical method of learning lines is in fact that 'chorus' system, repeating the speech through in sections, over and over again committing them to memory in short bursts, as it were. Then when you think you know it pretty well, cover each paragraph with an envelope as you proceed down the page and only look under it when you 'dry'. In this way you can memorise a speech perfectly.

Yet sometimes you will find that you know substantially what comes next but cannot immediately recall the exact words. This, oddly enough, is a good sign; gradually you may not bother to lift the envelope hiding the lines but plough on with slightly different phrasing which is still apt and in context. If you find it does not worry you that you are not sticking rigidly to the script but still making sense, you are on the way to being a very good speaker. Your mind carries on with still adequate vocabulary without the need for a prompt or a peek under the envelope. You are in control – splendid progress, provided you are not *lengthening* your speech in the process.

Mind you, that inspiration could well desert you on the night you make the speech for you always rehearse *without* the nerves attendant on the occasion. But practice does make perfect. If you can accustom yourself to think logically about each aspect of your speech you will be able to substitute, quite unconsciously, different and just as suitable phrases to make your point should the original lines escape you. You will be surprised how much easier it makes speech-making if you do not feel the need to be tied to a particular word each time. Sometimes you can delight yourself when on your feet by using a sudden, inspired phrase which has eluded you in the writing of the speech. But your mind must be attuned and sharp; it is not good rising full of wine and hoping to get by. Much better know the speech by heart in that case – and have notes to hand in the event of a befuddled dry.

I advise against actually reading speeches from fully written scripts. Only if it is a last-minute job or one demanding certain rigid protocol, should a speech ever be *read* to an audience. And if such an unenviable task falls your lot, write or type it on very firm, tough paper. Flimsy sheets can rustle in microphones and take off like a flock of pigeons in town hall draughts. Yet do not clip them together but leave them free so that when each page is completed you can lower it to the table below you. Get rid of used pages; do not try and slip them behind the wad in your hand. And if you should drop them during the final stages of the speech you do not have to search through the whole lot to find your place. Number the pages, of course, in case of such accidents. But keep 'read' speeches very short. If you rise holding what looks like the full manuscript of *Exodus* your audience will sink into a decline at once!

One cannot risk forgetting lines at state or civic occasions, but keep them down to one firm sheet of paper. If you have to turn pages you may get a nonsense as I once heard... *'I am greatly honoured to be here tonight...'* (turns two pages in error) ... *'but think the whole idea absurd.'* If such a gaffe happens it remains a big laugh or monumental black on a solemn occasion, to live forever in the minds of those organising the affair – and in yours.

If the occasion is reasonably informal and happy, then the read or parroted speech shows up to disadvantage against other speakers who, noteless and apparently impromptu, reel off bon mots, neat quips and anecdotes without any visible mental effort. However these seemingly off-the-cuff speeches and spontaneous wit are almost always the result of years of experience and rehearsal, rehearsal, rehearsal. Such speakers have stocked their minds, they can raid the larder any time they like and come up with something appetising for audiences. It is rarely true ad lib – it is the choice pickings from many past speeches.

Success does depend on rehearsal. Not in short breaks in your daily routine (although these naturally help as 'refreshers') but shut away from the family. Time and undivided attention must be given to rehearsal. Inexperienced speakers too often try to relegate speech preparation as a mere side-line to their daily round, while eating a meal, waiting for trains or between appointments at work. Others have ended in hospital trying to memorise lines at the wheel of a car. You must work on a speech like a professional actor, not fit it in life's odd moments. It is a known fact that the main cause for speeches going wrong is lack of rehearsal. Insufficient time has been spent on them and the speaker has relied on that curse of modern living, the banal hope of 'instant' success without having to work hard for it.

You can only train your memory if you allow it full and free scope in which to perform. Bother it by allowing subconscious side issues to disturb it, clutter it with extraneous matters during the learning of the words, and they will just not lodge permanently in your brain cells. A good memory is a bank into which you must pay something before you can draw any interest from it.

Use of Tape-Recorders for Learning

An excellent way of memorising lines – if it doesn't drive the rest of the family mad as you sit at your dressing table or shave in the bathroom with your own voice purring away at you, hour after hour. But you must shut yourself away with it, give it full concentration. And once you have finalised the speech do be sure to scrap all the tapes that include the early faults of enunciation, emphasis, over-long pauses or irregular breath control. When you have committed the speech to memory – or as far as you want to go in absorbing the bones of it so that you can extemporise at will – then use tape to see how you sound. But only when you are sounding fluent and balanced, your voice controlled and all accentuation and projection right, should you record a master tape to enable you finally to learn the lines.

Even then you can be in danger of sounding more like the tape than yourself, in other words, lose spontaneity in front of a 'live' audience through learning mechanically. On that final tape you must sound fresh, original and always as if the lines had just sprung to your mind. Only then will you make an impact as a personality beyond your subject.

But taping a speech is a good idea if you have the facilities. At least you know how you are going to sound, the timbre and pitch of your voice. And you will be able to eradicate any part that you feel sounds unwieldy, dull, monotonous – or insincere! Here again you must analyse yourself ruthlessly, you may love your own words, but you must assess them coldly as to how they will sound to a group of strangers – and you can surprise yourself how much you will cut out and replace. A tape recording should indicate to you the parts in your speech where you assume your audience knows you better than is possible, where, in fact, you have taken for granted your 'charm' will get you by – but, by listening dispassionately, you can hear that it won't!

Cue Cards
On the night of the speech leave the original script at home and take instead . . . cue cards. These can be ordinary white postcards or, if your sight is less than average, slightly larger. I cut out 6 in. x 4 in. oblong white surfaces from cartons or packages and those smooth cards supporting new shirts. With a thick black pen I write in block capitals, numbering the cue cards in the top right hand corner. And on them I write the 'cue' lines for each succeeding phase of my speech.

Now that I have rehearsed fully, I know the script and the running order like the back of my hand, I use the cue card to jog my memory on special phrases and vital links.

The first card, other than being headed by the date and name of function, I leave blank to be used for notes on the night. There is often a need to reply to other speaker's remarks or last-minute requests to mention something or somebody not in the original brief. I always find it easier to get shot of all these 'extra' inclusions as early as possible so that the fluency of your prepared speech is not impaired by unrehearsed insertions half way through.

Now here is an example of a set of cue cards.
1. 'Mr Chairman, ladies & gentlemen' (rest blank)
2. 'Thank for honour'
   Anecdote – mayor at town hall.
   Own qualifications
3. Shakespeare quote.
   Main theme
   Opposition's point of view
4. Interest within organisation
   Interest outside it – own viewpoint.
   Anecdote – christening ceremony.
5. Reference to chairman's golf handicap.
   Own golf anecdote.
   Wind-up – thank organisers.

As you study those cue card headings, you will say, quite rightly, 'those notes mean nothing to me' – and you are right. These references and anecdotes appear clueless – but not to the speaker who prepared them. He knows exactly what they refer to, he knows his own 'code' and so those cues are crystal clear as successive steps in his speech. To write them more fully is unnecessary. The object is to have quick visual cues that can trigger your memory off – if you should need them. They give you the running order and can be seen at a glance, rather than have to wade through paragraphs of material before you find your place. Also if you lost these cards no plagiarist could understand them!

If you happen to be prosposing a toast, it is advisable to mark the last card at the end *'Raise glass'*. When new to speaking it is forgivable if you sit down forgetting your brief to include in your speech – 'And now will you rise and drink the toast to our guests'. If you do, the chairman will have to prompt you, which can spoil the good impression you may have created. Of course if a toastmaster is employed he will boom forth: 'The toast is...' etc., but this ritual does waste valuable speaking time. I always feel that it's neat and economic if the speaker himself continues right into the toast. Forgetting your objective, too, can indicate that you are more conscious of yourself than the purpose of your speech.

Using such cue cards allows you more spontaneity; you can,

when experienced, ad lib with confidence, if the occasion demands, especially on previous speakers' statements. These you could not anticipate when preparing your speech, but sometimes they do need a reply. And the cue cards can keep you on the track of your rehearsed lines. Inserting last minute lines on a full script is never satisfactory. Your hasty scrawl becomes illegible and crawls away up the margin away from your normal eye line when on your feet.

That top blank card is useful for other speaker's names that you have not known before your arrived. Nothing improves the repose of a speech more than being able to, when illustrating a point on the theme of the evening to say, 'as Mrs Jones so rightly said just now . . .' It is a form of unrehearsed teamwork. The audience may not notice this fluidity – but they miss it if it is not there. If the whole function goes off smoothly with each speaker a contrasting character in a whole 'short' story, it has been highly successful.

As you gain in confidence you will find that, although you may make the same speech to different audiences many times, you will never give an identical performance, word for word, at each engagement. Despite the fact you may use the same cue cards, you will still improvise on the basic plot. Much as you relate an anecdote in a bar or at a party on the spur of the moment, so you will adopt this method in your social speeches. You have to be alert and not half-drunk, of course! But that approach does infuse naturalism in a speech which an audience enjoys. And you also need a good working vocabulary to do it.

So, having throughly learned your speech, discard the script and the tapes – and write out the cue cards. They will fit into handbags and pockets as easy memory refreshers on public transport and in quiet moments when you have some time to kill. But do not forget that you can only reach this standard by previous solid rehearsal in complete seclusion, devoid of other diversions.

Some speakers need notes more than others, but mostly because they have had too little time to rehearse or become easily bored by the practice. That attitude never produces a really imaginative speaker. There will be hesitations, a lot of 'ums' and 'ers', and slap-dash punctuation and pauses, minus any of the really creative thinking that can go into a well-rehearsed speech. It is always pleasing when going through a speech time and again, how you will add finer touches to your original words. Experienced speakers often never write a full script any more but begin with cue cards. They take them into a quiet room and merely rehearse versions of them.

One day you too may be able to do this. But don't try jumping the gun. Learn the speech in full first. Pre-speech nerves are set at rest if you know exactly what you are going to say and then you will only need the cue cards on the table beside the microphone.

Some speakers hide their cards behind propped-up menus at dinners and pretend to be speaking off the cuff! But if they do dry they have to reach down and turn them over which, if they have reached card 4 in their speech but No. 1 is still on top, causes a quite unnecessary pause while they sort through the pack. Don't be afraid of the audience seeing cue cards. And, if your speech has quite a few laughs in it, so design your cards that the last item on each is an amusing anecdote. Then, during the laugh, you have a good pause in which to turn to the next. However, don't *rely* on that laughter. Audiences are always unpredictable.

Cue cards provide an association of ideas upon which you can work entirely within your own character. They allow you to change your mood or approach to suit certain audiences. If faced with a boisterous lot you can adjust your style but, if tied by a speech learned by heart, you have little chance of changing. Thus, last minute attempts to inject some lighter – or more emotive – material can throw you and cause you to forget parts of the speech altogether.

In early days it might be as well to insert your bridging links on the cue cards but much depends how well you have rehearsed your speech. These should have become first nature before you even reach the cue card stage.

Relevant bridging links are a great value in helping you to learn your lines. But if you write your speech with every paragraph unrelated or as a *non sequita*, then a speech is not easy to memorise. Most speech learning is done by 'fixation' or 'relationship' so that a sequence is absorbed in the mind, one word automatically jogging your memory for the next. For instance, you may mention 'wine' in a dinner speech; this 'reminds' you to tell a drunk story. 'Motor roads' leads you to an anecdote of a friend caught for speeding, and so on, always an association of ideas. However, there is no real artifice which can replace good rehearsal and a clear memory. Cultivate this and half your nerves will be gone.

Young people have good retentive memories – unless they are on the drug scene which begins its killing in the mind – but older people sometimes find memorising more difficult simply because they have absorbed more into their brain cells in living longer and room has to be made for storage space. Most veteran speakers, having logged up thousand of speaking hours in the oral orbit, do not wilt or become unnerved if their material momentarily leaves them. They pause, take stock of their notes, then resume with an aplomb not yet acquired by a beginner.

I have heard this. A seventy-five year old speaker suddenly paused. 'Macbeth was played by . . . let me see . . . who was that Hollywood actor?' Someone shouted 'Orson Welles'. 'That's the chap,' said the unperturbed oldster. His absolute confidence was thoroughly enjoyed by the audience. But a novice might well have stuttered, gone grey and, despite having begun the anecdote, abandoned it in sheer terror.

Filing System for Cue Cards

Head the top cue card with date, functions and subject of speech so that you can file them away for quick reference. As you progress in the speaking world, you are often called upon at short notice so have your cards always available.

After a speech I usually mark the cards 'Yes' and 'No' against each item. That means I used, or did not use, certain items so that, if called upon to speak at that date again, I know which material they have already heard and that which will still be fresh to them on a possible return date.

Also I mark items on the cards which were not successful, the anecdotes which missed the target or quotations which did not quite come off. This does not mean I discard them entirely, but that I can work on them with more detailed consideration. You will find, as you grow in public speaking experience, that you will use favourite phrases, pet similes, anecdotes or quotations with which you will persevere despite some audiences not appreciating them. I am not talking about any remark liable to offend or bring gasps of astonishment but points which, within yourself, you know to be bright, witty or apt, and yet still do not appeal as you feel they should. But you plod on with them, trying to find the right format, the right presentation. And one day it happens. The audience rises to them with the right wave of approbation. At last you have the right phrasing, timing and presentation. Then you are glad you marked your cue card to work on it, rather than abandon it after one fruitless attempt.

Very often it is a question of re-writing, changing the order of events. You may be ending on the wrong aspect, giving the game away too early or stressing the obvious. When you revise any aspect of speech-making, always work on the premise of maintaining the mystery as long as you can, especially when a surprise ending is your aim. Your final line must have the impact of climax, not a lame explanation of your previous sentence.

'Off-The-Cuff' Speaking

If you hear a splendid 'ad lib' speech without notes, you will know two things about the speaker. He is vastly experienced and his 'spontaneous' remarks are, as I mentioned earlier, the result of years of rehearsal. He or she has reached a point in their careers when, undaunted by nerves any more, they can rake through their mind for appropriate material from the hundreds of speeches they have made. They even have set 'ad lib' retorts for interrupters which sound extremely bright and clever but, in reality, have been used hundreds of times before.

One develops an instinct for such speeches, especially when the audience knows you are a late choice, taking someone else's place at the last minute. They little realise you have a filing system and can trot out a speech at the drop of a hat! A 'short-notice' speech can be delightful challenge when you've been on the speaking scene a few years ... simply because you know that you *start* with the sympathy of the audience!

But the rambling speech from the 'I never need notes' waffler is often a sign of laziness and a cavalier approach to audiences rather than a sign of superior intellect. 'I just stand up and say what comes into my head,' he boasts. Yet he is inevitably the dullest speaker in the whole round-up. Immersed in his own self-importance, he meanders, side-tracks, chuckles and ruminates through his remarks absolutely convinced that his near pointless words are genius. He never sticks to time limits. No sir, that's for other speakers. Once on his feet he takes root. Often such people are big fish in small ponds, many of whom may hold our careers in their cold fins so they have to be tolerated.

They only delude themselves of course; we laugh at them behind their backs. They can never capitalise on their luck of supreme self-confidence. They cannot be bothered to prepare a succinct, pithy speech in which their undoubted knowledge could be properly harnessed and strengthened by tight editing. Only the professional entertainer knows when an audience wants to be 'milked', that is, give them their moneys worth from a box office point of view. But the amateur who tries to 'milk' an audience by long-windedness with unprepared speeches full of repetition and no sense of time has no real place on a public rostrum.

So use a filing system and have a set speech up your sleeve in case of emergency. You must, however, always ensure that you are technically right both in delivery and material. It is not a question of getting away with charm, an engaging manner or downright cheek; you must have good material and your mind sufficiently creative to deal with it effectively. Kissing the Blarney Stone is supposed to give you power to speak well in public – but some perhaps speak more blarney than sense.

Summary of LEARNING A SPEECH AND USING NOTES
1. Beware of parrot-fashion learning taking the personality out of delivery.
2. Try learning by ad lib technique.
3. Never take fully-written script manuscripts to a speaking date.
4. Use Cue Cards and allow for improvisation within your subject.
5. Work with a tape-recorder if it is available.
6. File your cue cards systematically for future speeches, after marking them with 'success' or 'failure' notes.
7. Always have an all-purpose speech up your sleeve.

CHAPTER SIX

Humour in Speeches

One of the biggest disasters to strike the western world in the
'fifties' was the sudden, rapid decline in a sense of humour. The
advent of the 'sick' joke, 'black' comedy and the filthy story
told in public, even on television, evidenced that a sense of true
fun had ebbed out of people. With permissiveness, humour was
now used to affront, to dare to say what no man or woman
had dared to say in public before. No longer could optimism
be instilled, the wry humour of seeing 'the funny side' of bad
luck; instead people became indignant or outraged, the
malaise of the materialistic. Laughter today is too often equated
with derision and mockery – mainly of those unable to
hit back – rather than in a happy sense of the ridiculous, the
pantomime of the absurd and scintillating wit of alert
minds.

In his book 'The Nature of Laughter' Max Eastman wrote:
'Laughter is the exorcism of misfortune'. If he is right – and I
am sure he is – then we can easily understand why we live in
such a gloomy, suspicious, uptight, belligerent world today.
Someone has forgotten to pass on to current youth the joy of
pure laughter. What has happened to that expanse of character
which once allowed us to laugh at ourselves? As I write, many
citizens categorise humour as the prerogative of the showbusiness
comedians but not part of *normal* living. Laughter is 'reserved'
for special occasions, TV, stage farces, cabaret and club comics
– but few people ever *provide it for themselves* any more in
conversation. They would no more think of spontaneous
laughter at their job – or, even more tragically – in their home
– than they would chuckle at their mother's funeral. Lack of

domestic fun must have helped break up many homes and certainly widened the generation gap.

Even hard-hit Victorian slums had street corner comedy although, God knows, there was far less leisure then today. Yet somehow they managed to find laughter. It was their loom of unquenchable enthusiasm, unconquerable personality and enduring hope. It was a way of life, not relegated to time and place as today. Every shop, factory and office had its comic, stranger could rib stranger and street dialogue was spiced with badinage and wisecrack. And let no argument say it was childish – it saved reason and pride – as it did later, for servicemen and women in wars.

Now, as we no longer whistle in the street, so have we forgotten the gift of unsophisticated laughter. Blame what you will, the car, radio, television, greed, we have lost our most valuable asset. The rich guffaws of uninhibited laughter once heard over neighbouring garden walls have been demolished with those garden walls.

You, as a public speaker, have a choice – to be the one who likes to raise laughter or the other who prefers to remain serious in approach. And I would rather you remain that sort of horse for a course than attempt comedy without any real finesse or flair for it.

Many public speaking tutors do not see humour as having a really prominent place in speech-making. Certainly they devote little time or space to it. But, humbly, I disagree. Make an audience laugh with genuine humour and they cannot dislike you – and will be far more ready to listen to argument if it is couched in well-turned amusing phrases. The reason why so many despise humour as a speech ingredient worthy of special attention is that it is by far the most difficult technique of all in public speaking. Most solemn instructors do, I am sure, have a sour grapes attitude towards it. But we must have laughter somewhere along the modern rocky roads. At least if your speech raises laughter it will be remembered long after those of the very real and earnest pundits.

Comedy in public speaking does not mean that you rely entirely on joke or anecdote. Both have their place, but have to be properly told and timed. That is why many amateur, self-styled, red-nosed comics wonder what's hit them when they steal and re-tell a string of a professional's best jokes – and find they die a silent death in a speech. One needs considerable expertise to make people laugh in public – that is, laugh *with* you, not *at* your doleful attempts to be funny.

Not even if we look funny, are we naturally funny people! That is why humour must be treated within the compass of your own personality. Many alleged comics try too hard and rarely rehearse with correct timing, repose or lucid projections. They think they know it all, can do it naturally, be 'instant successes'. So they tell a story in a speech as they would in a bar – 'There was this bird, see . . .' completely without timing, technique or relevancy. Oh, it may get laughs from some shallow-minded audiences, but never to the whole-hearted degree as when it is intricately woven into the fabric of the speech and a similar care has been taken in its presentation.

Television comedians make it look easy, but it remains a very artistic craft needing, above all, that elusive gift of timing. Why is that even some experienced speakers just cannot make a particular joke seem funny? Because in their mouths it is incongruous. They do not make themselves part of it, they tell it as they heard it, in an *isolated* way. They have 'cracked it' because it is a joke – not selected it assiduously as being absolutely *their* sort of joke, suiting their image. They do not pay themselves the compliment of adapting the story, which with time and trouble they could, to make it seem logical part of their character – just as professional comedians do!

A practised humorous speaker becomes very adroit at re-writing stories from their original context to suit his speeches. A story about a bishop in a railway compartment can be refurbished to become a director in a boardroom or an admiral in a wardroom. As you gain experience this improvisation can become second-nature, and you will listen intently for every passing remark. As, for example, one I picked up when I was writing this book. A dear old Mrs Malaprop told me her grandson was at a difficult age and 'going through a *phrase*'. I turned this to useful account when speaking at a ladies' literary lunch, changing the central character from female to male – with an all-woman audience that was tactful!

There is a time and place to tell a story which would be woefully wrong on other occasions. Some speakers, having heard a professional stage, television or club entertainer tell a gag, immediately use it at a lunch, dinner or in a lecture hall. They do not analyse the difference in audiences. The professional has a relaxed lot and the atmosphere in his theatre is entirely different. They have paid to be entertained, that is their sole purpose for queuing at the box office. But the lunch, dinner or town hall audience does not integrate quite so solidly. All members still retain a feeling of personal importance to the occasion which they would lose in the darkness of a theatre.

Also a speaker does not do an 'act' – or shouldn't, although the speeches of many amateur comics are nothing more. The art of the humorous speech is that it *remains* a speech, moulded to the theme of the evening with every remark pertinent to the occasion. And if you can achieve that, your date book will be very full indeed.

No person ever admits that they do not possess a sense of humour. Yet, sadly, far less do than don't. Some have a limited range. From slapstick to sarcasm, humour covers a wide range of emotional reaction. As a person cannot stand one particular comedian and yet weep with laughter at another, so his neighbour reverses the preferences. But both comedians have their share of public acclaim. So in public speaking you will have to choose the entertainment you provide carefully to suit both your personality – and your audience. A speech made to medical students is unlikely to appeal to a church hall audience.

But, you will say, how can I find out what an audience is like if I am a stranger to that particular engagement? The answer in early speaking is make your humour match the subject of your speech. But, as the years pass, you will find you get a nose for an audience. You can, after moving around in the chat race for a while, assess the type it will be. You can judge from the invitation who is likely to be listening to you, the ordinary man in the street or a specialised society. That audience will know your theme – so you aim to make them laugh *within* it. So long as your humour has point, a sense of direction and is unlikely to offend, you will never be far off target.

Basically humour is appreciating life's ironies as they manifest themselves both in our own and other people's lives. There is the laughter of misinterpretation and ignorance, impudence giving dignity a kick in the pants, the guile of greed going wrong – and the more limited sardonic humour which warps the most innocent situations by acid wit. And of course these filthy joke addicts to whom nothing, repeat nothing, is funny in their estimation unless it has lavatorial or sexual overtones. To similar moronic citizens derision, goading and harassment of others is 'funny'. They use ridicule as a form of vendetta against anyone outside their own ken instead of more sensibly learning from them. That is, miserably, part of the growing trend of vandalism among the young, the desire to destroy anything that gives pleasure to others. 'I broke down that young tree, didn't I, just for giggle.' How the sudden popularity of 'giggle' in teenage vocabulary symbolises the low standard of humour in our times!

So if you aim to give us happy, unrestricted laughter in your speeches, bless you for trying. But do it well, or not at all.

Good Taste in Humour

Sounds pompous, but it is not intended to be. Humour is as prickly an aspect of public speeches as politics. As a stage comedian does, you should try to please the majority of your audience even if you can't please them all. Too often speakers, in their early speeches, are content just to make their particular friends laugh regardless of the fact that the main body of the room does not appreciate their brand of comedy. However trendy a speaker may feel, it is a poor tactic in the speaking business. If you know you will offend the susceptibilities of the majority by your approach, avoid it. If your conception of humour is so limited then there must be occasions when you should not try to be funny at all. It is common-sense. Why make enemies?

Brash speakers will sometimes purposely denigrate religion simply because there are some clerics in the room and they feel their cronies will adore them for embarrassing the cloth. This is an adolescent ploy. Most churchmen cope very easily with such bad manners. But where the speakers also let themselves down is that, on such occasions, the audience watch the reaction of the clerics rather than interest themselves in the speech. Knocking any establishment is a popular gimmick in early speech-making but, believe me, it will get you nowhere in the end.

When such attempts are made by 'progressives' lampooning established beliefs, the instigators are always more indignant that it falls flat than those to whom the jibes are aimed. Yet the Churches are still a fund of a great many hilarious stories perfectly acceptable even to archbishops and nuns. But a religion is every man's inheritance. Some disdain to accept it while others guard it as their most prized possession. All speakers should treat it with respect for it involves man's most secret self . . . so 'do unto others as you would they do unto you . . .'

Other sensitive channels of humour are 'child-birth', 'death' and 'afflictions'. Funeral and death-bed jokes are mainly 'sick' although a few in a limited way can be amusing. But if you are sitting in that audience having just lost a loved one, whether you are an 'ancient' or a 'modern', you are not going to laugh. Nor will you if your skin pigmentation or creed is being held to ridicule in public with you its lone representative in the room. The Jewish race always scores in public speaking with stories against itself. It is a magnificent form of defence – and no non-Jewish speaker in his right mind would ever attempt to follow them with similar stories. And, in the fullness of time, other castes and creeds will follow suit – as indeed now when coloured club comedians are so refreshingly funny adapting the 'Raj' prejudices to their own to raise laughs. Where they, too, have to be careful during the tetchy transitionary period of understanding, is that they do not pick at the already healing sores and open them up again. One can overbalance a professional 'tolerance' too far on the other side.

So, with your humour, respect your audience's intelligence. Use wit without excretia, keep your fun on an expansive plane rather than narrowed into trends. Speakers who aim to get laughs need also to keep their friends . . .

Using a Funny Story

When you collect stories for speeches, file them under their respective headings. It is surprising how, with ingenuity, many can be used to suit dozens of occasions beyond the obvious background of the original joke. Analyse the story, find its basic ingredients, and break it down, component by component. Let's use this odd throwaway which I have adapted successfully many times.

'A neighbour of mine complained bitterly about living on our busy main road. Walking home from the station at night was a menace because of the heavy speeding traffic. But he found the answer.

'Wear white,' he told me. 'A white hat, white coat and white wellingtons. Then the drivers are bound to see you.'

A week later I heard he was in hospital after a street accident so I went to see him. He was covered in bandages and had a leg in plaster.

'What on earth happened?' I asked, 'were you wearing your all-white outfit?'

'Yes,' he sighed, 'but I was run over by a snow-plough . . .'

Now when I first heard that, the teller said the chap had been run over – *and killed* – a quite unnecessary, chilling buffer to full laughter at the end. Told that way in public, someone might have lost a relative in a car crash, So the death angle I cut out straight away thus *widening* its value.

Look at the story again. Into what categories could you put it?

'Clothing' is one aspect. 'Traffic', 'Neighbours', 'Hospitals'. I have heard it used at weddings when the bride wore white. It can be used similarly at tennis or cricket functions where 'white' is the playing garb. Then it comes under headings like 'Optimism', 'Inventiveness', 'Ingenuity', 'Do-It-Yourself' and even that 'whiter-than-white' advertising slogan. The only time not to tell it is when the snow lies thick outside so that the audience may well anticipate the end!

Another example of breaking down a story is this:

'My son was amazed when I told him that, when I was his age there was no television in the home at all.

'But dad,' he said, 'I've always visualised your youth as being at least in black and white . . .'

Short but useful, under headings like 'Television', 'Children', 'Family Life', 'Looking Back', 'Being Out of Date', 'Passing Time'. Such an anecdote is an ideal bridging link in itself.

Once while washing-up my wife broke a cup. 'That,' she said furiously, 'means I've got another saucer I've no use for.'

I turned that into an after-dinner speech 'throw-away' too.

Domestic incidents like that are extremely valuable. This deals with the less obvious aspect of a normal household breakage. Housewives always enjoy it, including my dutiful wife who has heard me tell it dozens of times. When I asked her why she still laughed herself, she said : 'I like watching the faces of those who haven't heard it . . . their reaction of surprise is always so pleasing.' Which, bless her, sums up humour in speeches. Anticipation and surprise. And that anecdote can offend no one.

Of course when she made the original remark she had been entirely serious – and that is how such anecdotes grow – out of real life. They do not necessarily begin as a laugh. That is the difference between the anecdote and the outlandish situation joke which may well rely on a 'fantasy' backgrounds like the Pearly Gates or mermaids in the first place. People are more apt to enjoy the funny side of a normal occurrence in our daily round. Rather like the old music hall gag of the man, who for sake of economy, bought himself a new suit with one jacket and two pairs of trousers – and promptly burned a hole in the coat! This must have happened to someone in real life in times of dire poverty when such an accident was sheer disaster. But in the end it was handed on to raise a laugh. Which is what humour is about.

So, when you hear a presentable story, write it down first and then study it for all its potentials. Can it be used beyond its obvious category? Can you by a change of character or environment use it in a wider or even more subtle context? It is a fascinating exercise, sometimes resulting in only the original pay-off line remaining from the original story – and most people will think it entirely new!

Never use the tactic of adapting a real person into a funny story. It used to be be a popular dinner gimmick and keeps getting reinvented. You hear a joke and, later in a speech, you tell it as a real life story about one of the guests present. It may sound harmless enough but it is highly dangerous. I have seen much embarrassment caused by this quite unnecessary ploy, especially if the joke was also a dirty one into the bargain. In one case it was a gag about a man, named in the speech, going to bed with his wife. The guest who was made the fall guy just walked quietly out of the room. The speaker looked annoyed – 'Only a joke,' he sneered, 'can't he take it?' 'Could you?' said the chairman, 'if the wife you once went to bed with died only a few months ago?' We were all glad when that dinner was over.

Certainly use anecdotes about authentic people – but never put them in as characters in fictitious jokes. It is poor presentation, and as nobody believes it anyway, why waste time on it? All 'jokes' must be about third persons, not friends – or even foes!

Telling a Funny Story

Rehearse it. Don't rely on the version you ad lib in the pub or club. Your speech audience is in a different mood, you have to project your voice, use more volume to reach them and they are not all old established chums tolerant of your haphazard style.

Write it out, for amateur raconteurs so often over-elaborate jokes by flooding the facts with their own exuberance. Edit it to its concise form. When you hear joke-tellers meandering along you can guess that on their cue cards or notes they have just marked 'court-room story' and suddenly lapse from the rehearsed section of their speech into a hesitant tavern style to tell an ad lib joke. Jokes must be *rehearsed*, especially for timing. After all, raising laughter is never easy. Other parts of your speeches may please or displease but you will never know. But if the laughter does not come at the end of your comedy, you look a right chump ... So a story should be rehearsed with, if anything, even more detailed concentration than the rest of a speech.

Usually amateur joke-tellers change their speaking pace when they reach their 'funnies'. They quicken up and gabble rather than maintain the steadier delivery of the preceding sentences. So he changes his image to the bewilderment of the audience ... a sort of Dr Jeykell and Mr Hyde transformation – heralding the fact that he is NOW GOING TO BE FUNNY which stiffens up most audiences to make them all the harder to break down.

While brevity is necessary some speakers, however, do tell a story too baldly, completely without characterisation or colour. 'A tramp knocked on a rich man's door...' This sort of bare outline gives the audience little chance to 'see' the picture in their mind. But 'the hungry old tramp looked at the glistening white front door, then raised the big brass knocker . . .' does create a real picture. 'Rich' is a crude term and the opulence is better implied by the description of the door. This is not over-elaborating but infusing atmosphere into the story. You are not going off at tangents or including irrelevant detail, the story is progressing to its climax all the time, but in an interesting way.

Again, if you begin a story . . . 'My neighbour, about my age, is a keen football fan . . .' that may be all you need to establish him for the sake of the climax. Add the information that he once had a trial for the Arsenal, played for the local village, was a widower and drank rather heavily, if none of these facets are vital to the pay-off, you only confuse the audience with such a build-up. It is sad how many speakers either over-embroider stories with completely irrelevant data in the mistaken impression they are setting a colourful scene or else tell it so flatly that it has no human interest at all. You have to make your description progressive in all anecdotes . . . every word must take the story onward. If you were directing a film and your central characters were speeding along a Dutch road, being chased by crooks, you would not suddenly use a close-up of a windmill simply because you like windmills. Unless it played an important part in that action, it would slip by in a flash.

The true raconteur 'sees' the story in his mind as he tells it, very like using a film camera. Challenge him in mid-story as to what his characters were wearing and, although clothing has nothing to do with the story, he or she could tell you in detail. When I tell a story in public I visualise the entire scene, even to a nearby lamp-post – but I don't mention it's there unless it is needed in the story development. It is not a knack, but just a question of thinking creatively. That is why rehearsal is so necessary – it attunes your mind to create the atmosphere.

While a story may be fiction, it is, in the telling, a passing *fact* in your mind. If you use the radio technique it should allow audiences to listen in that way, the words allowing them to form their own mind pictures of the plot development. That is why radio is so much more stimulating as an exercise for the brain than television. You can play a part yourself rather than just sit back and let the box do it all for you.

If you have not thought of story-telling on these lines before, the best training I can offer is to think of your anecdotes in the *present* tense, as *about* to happen. This gives them more pungency than quoting them merely as past history. So, much as you see a 'repeat' on television of a programme you have already seen before, you tell a story – just as if it was happening all over again rather than just a report of a bygone incident. That gives it a freshness, a crispness of authenticity, especially with anecdotes and you will be surprised at the blood transfusion you can give it. And told in this manner your story will also sound an integral part of your speech rather than a disjointed insertion.

The way not to tell jokes in speeches is again the bar technique of 'Have you heard about the man . . .' Never raise a story by that hoary old system in a speech. Someone might shout out . . . 'Yes, we have!' Never ask questions of an audience in light-hearted speeches, anyway, for they love participating! And, too, if you have not written the joke out first but rely on off the cuff memory – you may say: 'Have you heard the one about the man who picked up the wrong hat in a restaurant . . .' As the joke relies, for its surprise ending, on the fact that the man has the wrong hat, you have wrecked the tag-line by telling the end first!

This can happen to items even in serious speech-making. Bad speech construction will give the game away too early, the plot is revealed long before the climax so that all interest is killed. A speech must be written to maintain the mystery so that your final line has it fullest impact.

You will have to be very experienced to get away with being the witty one yourself in anecdotes. In any case the approach will be obviously contrived to show the audience just how clever you are. By all means use your own *observation* in neat turns of phrase, but it takes a great deal of skill to be convincing as the winner in anecdotes you, yourself, recount. The risk is sounding too smart, too self-assured.

And don't laugh when you are telling stories! Second-rate club comics do this, hoping their own side-splitting mirth will give the gag impetus to galvanise the food-and-drink-satiated audience. Mark you, it is hard to enforce the no laughter rule. I have good friends who become so tickled when they begin a story that they chuckle their way through, wiping their eyes and often kill the tag line by their own merriment making it entirely incomprehensible. However, unless the audience is very grim indeed, they, too, are usually reduced to similar hysterics simply because the speaker's own laughter is so absurdly infectious. By all means smile if you want to – but the funniest stories are told with a dead pan. The best laughs are gained by 'surprise'.

Use of Anecdotes and Quotations

Provided you have your facts right certainly use anecdotes about real people. They are of far more value to a speech than a joke because they are true and far more likely to be apposite to the theme. While anecdotes would not go well in a stage act, they certainly improve a public speech. As Jack Benny once said on television : 'Truth is funnier than fiction . . .'

There are books in your library on quotable 'quotes' and anecdotes, besides those you can find in newspapers and magazines, although I remind you once again that those heard on television do have such a vast coverage that it as well to note them down and pull them into cold storage for a much later date.

Always acknowledge your source of course. Never pretend an anecdote happened to you personally if it is a lie . . . this dangerous practice leads to a most embarrassing unmasking, sooner or later, by someone more informed than the average who can make you look pretty small in public.

Children's sayings are extremely useful speech fodder as they always work well in normal light-hearted functions.

But I do appreciate that hearing anecdotes – or even new jokes – around the social scene is almost a thing of the past, especially among young people. Maybe the juke box drowns the dialogue, perhaps we are too wrapped up in our own mazed thoughts to want to discuss others. But it is a sad fact of modern life that anecdotes are not exchanged as once they were.

It is certainly evident in my own world. Showbusiness was perhaps the greatest source of anecdote once, being full of bizarre and extrovert characters – but today alas no more. Once we toured in plays and musicals, not as the one or two who manage to find theatres do now, but in dozens to every town in the country. So, thrust on each other's company for months on end we exchanged laughter, stories about our respective landladies in our 'digs' and handed on traditional stories of other actors who had gone before us. Television and radio have no such backstage life. You arrive for rehearsals much as if you worked in a bank and knock off at a set time – and go home. If you do not actually play a scene with someone in the company, you may never even meet them for they are pre-filmed on different days from you. So there is nothing like the chance of making new friendships or exchange of conversation there once was – and so no off-stage personalities grow up among the players.

This sad state of affairs reflects in other walks of life too. The computor replaces an office staff. The car with its solitary occupant, commuter trains packed like sardines – people come home exhausted. So is bred a reticence. Conversation in the home is restricted by the telly and some thin-thinking people now cannot live without it. For lonely people it may be a god-send, but they are only lonely because no one talks to them and if the truth be known they would prefer a visitor sometimes to allow them to use their own personality and contribute dialogue themselves.

This state of affairs caused me an interesting dilemma once. I was asked to give a professional 'talk' in the west country on 'Theatre Humour'. Beginning in Victorian times I traced, by means of anecdote, the evolution of stage comedy. It was a success. The mixed audience of all ages laughed and, to my pride and everlasting gratitude, stood to me as I sat down. With this 'triumph' under my belt, I went off to the midlands to make the same speech to another but much younger association.

My first six minutes left them absolutely cold. Nary a laugh. What had gone wrong? The west country had enjoyed it. Then a strange thought struck me. I was talking about the past – and this young audience just did not want to know about it. They were not interested in humour at all, let alone how it developed. So, if I was to please my audience, I had to forget my main theme.

So I switched, not my anecdotes, but the names of the

central characters in them, breaking my own golden rule for the sake of sheer diplomacy. For Harry Tate, I quoted Jimmy Edwards, Jimmy Tarbuck surplanted Robb Wilton, Dan Leno turned into Harry Secombe – and immediately the room was rolling with laughter!

Instead of following the original script I had to start 'modern' and stay there. Normally I reached 'present day' half way through, rounding off the last ten minutes with the Goon humour of Spike Milligan, Michael Bentine and Peter Sellers – but, on this occasion, they had to lead the field as past stars were just not accepted by that audience. In their estimation no dead man or woman could have been funny. The sole prerogative belonged to their generation alone. That attitude meant that their humour lacked true spontaneity; they put a time and place on it, regulated it like turning a tap on and off.

It is difficult to assess. Frankly, if you enjoy a laugh it does not matter whether the characters in an anecdote are alive or dead, provided the basic plot is funny. And this I proved in the character switch. To become obsessed with the present is just as restricting as living in the past. Because a scene belongs to a previous generation does not mean that it is valueless; otherwise, logically, we would have to scrap yesterday's plan at every new dawn.

Now I have considerably rewritten that 'talk' – and pick my audiences very carefully indeed. Certainly you should use anecdote all you can, but don't take a leaf out of my book in this instance and alter names just to sound trendy. I did it in an emergency to save getting egg on my face but I am more cunning now! I begin in the present and go backwards. In that way I pose the question 'what will this young generation leave for posterity in its laughter?' As they care very much about that and don't want it forgotten, they now seem to enjoy it.

The trouble with up-dating a true anecdote by altering its personnel is that someone in the audience may know the true story. I once heard a young speaker anecdoting about Yorkshire cricket to be interruped by an irate veteran who bawled: 'That was not Freddie Truman, it was Abe Waddington – before you were born, lad!' The room went quiet and the boy stumbled on awkwardly, no longer reliable in the audience's eyes.

So, as in other points of speech, get your facts right even in anecdotes. They do enliven any sort of talk, for they serve to illustrate points 'scenically' rather than the bald statement of fact, adding weight to, and often justifying, your own opinions. But keep your sense of perspective. Don't quote Winston Churchill's 'blood, toil, tears and sweat' speech when you referring to the building of a new scout hut . . . !

Collect the personal anecdote all you can and listen all the time. It need not be about V.I.Ps but ordinary people – in fact these make the most valuable anecdotes of all.

My father, when travelling round England gathering architectural data for a lecture tour of America, found himself at a Gloucestershire village church. Cutting the hedge was the sexton. Father said: 'Beautiful old church.' The man replied with a sigh: 'Aye, the church is all right – the trouble is they will put a parson in it.'

Ever since that long-gone day that remark has been used in all sorts of contexts, by my father on that U.S.A. lecture tour, by me in speeches and in a novel – and by countless amused churchmen themselves whom I have seen make a note of it when I have been on my feet. That anecdote possesses that glorious ingredient, the underdog taking a pertinent crack at the establishment. But I must warn all 'progressive moderns' who might be tempted to use it – the incident took place in 1924! You see? Does it matter when it happened?

Such personal anecdotes do not remain your sole property for long in the speaking world if they are as adaptable as that one is. But do try and find your own if you can. I realise it is not so easy in the restricted community relationships today. We have lost so much opportunity. Once shipboard travel was a treasure trove of ideas when people struck up temporary friendships at the deck rail. Now they strap us in a plane. It saves time but stifles exchange of ideas. If you place any value on public speaking humour, you need to go out and about and meet people, not let machines make all the sounds you hear.

Reminiscences
These are closely related to the anecdote, but usually are applied to pay tribute to some particular personality in your speech.

Often they are actually in the room listening to you, perhaps waiting to speak themselves.

Some speech trainers hate speakers who reminisce. Personally I enjoy good recollections if they are valid and not drawn out. The trouble with personal memories, like jokes, is that the speaker tends not to write them out first in the speech but dwells upon them in nostalgic ad lib and so become clogged with sides issues . . .

'I well remember Fred, he was married to Joe's cousin, Lucy, whose father kept "The Lamb & Flag" at Launceston, next door to George Jackson's grocer shop where Harry Smith was a counter-hand before Charlie Roberts took over . . .'

By the time Fred reappears in the speech the audience doesn't know, or care, whether he was a grocer or a lamb!

So treat reminiscence as you would a joke or anecdote. Make it snappy. Weed out irrelevant data . . . who cares if Fred was married, single or had ambitions to be Pope? If these aspects have nothing to do with the point you wish to illustrate, cut them out. The answer is rehearsal – and disciplined speaking from a clear-cut rather than a wandering mind.

Use of Dialect in Stories

If you possess a dialect of your own use it to advantage. Your stories will have an authentic touch and a dialect story is always a neat diversion if properly presented in a speech – and provides valuable contrast.

But never, please, stand up and say to an audience: 'I can't do the Irish accent but there was this Paddy . . .' That is a certain sign of the brash beginner . . . you are offering the audience a third-rate version, you are apologising for being incompetent, you are telling them, point blank, you are not the right horse for the course. If you cannot create the true atmosphere, then don't tell the story. It is as simple as that. No story is so good that it cannot be left out especially if you cannot do it justice.

You may well consider it during rehearsal and see if it cannot be adapted to a brogue you can imitate to the life. But do not, I beg you, fuddle through on a sketchy attempt. It is an insult to your audience and shows you up as lacking in judgement.

Now some of us can 'pass muster' at certain dialects. We are sufficiently versed in them to give an adequate representation in short spells, but we could never sustain a big role on stage in that dialect. If the story is short we can usually get away with a sane attempt to create the dialect. But in a long story, no. Never tell long stories in speeches anyway.

Try telling a Welsh story to an audience containing Welshmen! If you are not from their green valleys, my God, man, they will let you know! Dialects, like religions, are an inheritance that sons of certain shores hold most possessively. They can easily be offended by some foreigner making a mockery of their precious speech. They certainly won't laugh at the joke, that's for certain, and if they happen to be on the speaking bill with you, when they rise they can make you look a prize idiot when *they* start stories in their natural dialect!

The novice usually resorts to the 'catch-phrase' device in dialects instead of imparting the true intonation. 'Bejabers' for Irish, 'Och aye' for Scots, 'Look you' for Welsh, 'Gaw blimey' for Cockney, 'Yoi, yoi' for Jewish . . . Just try 'Good on yer, sport' if you are not Australian – but some in your audience are!

No, lay off dialects you do not know and select stories within your range. And if you do not know any dialects, play straight, be yourself and tell stories in your own voice. For, within that, you know you have all the control, natural inflection and emphasis to get the best out of a story. Forcing yourself into an unaccustomed dialect will lose you proper timing and correct accentuation anyway. And there is always the danger of straining the voice box.

If you are methodical in sorting your collected material you need never risk exceeding your limitations. But if you lack application and are content to make a speech which haphazardly includes the last six stories you heard around town, you will be speaking from a muddled mind, cluttered with half-formed phrases and your delivery will suffer. You may think you appear 'nice 'n easy', 'casual-like' – but it will be a hell to listen to – and your very unpreparedness is not a compliment to a discerning audience.

Blue Jokes
You have to be very sure of your audience to tell dirty jokes in public and frankly I advise against it strongly. However

much you might amuse a certain minority, a reliance entirely upon dirt shows up a terrible mental limitation. I am not a prude but I don't like mucky gags in speeches. The double entendre, the risqué, in their proper place, can be splendid entertainment – but downright filth, never.

Yet there are those I mentioned earlier who feel nothing can be funny unless it is about sex or lavatories. Some speakers also think it 'trendy' to be 'blue' and, God help us, do not actually know the difference between a risqué story which never uses a dubious word and the really digusting story full of four letter muck. To them both jokes are synonymous and if one speaker uses a clever double entendre, the blue comic accepts it as a 'filthy story' precedent and so follows it with sheer excretia! It happens a lot at sports dinners and, when reprimanded, the comedian accuses the previous speaker of starting it! Alas, for the ignorance of being unable to see the dividing line between wit and manure.

As any professional entertainer will tell you, the cheapest way to raise laughs is by being 'blue'. But the real test – and by far the most satisfying – is when you can please an audience with clean material. As one who has appeared at police concerts, possibly the 'bluest' night in any professional's year when the dirt rolls thick and fast, it can be both nauseating and degrading. Usually at such functions the waitresses are sent out of the room by the chairman, in itself a puerile way for men to behave in public.

You know yourself and your audiences best. I am not the high priest of purity but I do know the really blue joke has no place in decent public speaking. Take the case of the mature lady mayoress of a town some years ago. Poor dear, she tried to be 'mod' and 'with-it' so, at the annual town hall dinner she told her good citizens a dirty story, roughly as follows:

'Two R.A.F. pilots during the war, took two girls in secret on a flight over enemy territory. They were shot up and with the machine in flames one officer said to the other: "There's only two parachutes. What do we do with the girls?'

'F—— 'em.'

'Have we got time?'

Quite naturally the parochial audience took strong exception to their lady mayoress and her idea of an after-dinner joke.

Certainly it could hardly have been relevant to her theme! And of course the story reached the national press. What is so sad is, that story was not particularly funny *anyway* ... not even on an alcoholic stag night. Most sports clubs could do better with less offence. If that mayoress had done her homework properly – and the war *was* her subject – this is the story she could have told:

'Two Land Army girls had a night on the town and crept back to their hostel in the small hours. They had to climb barbed wire, scale a wall and roof to get back into their quarters undetected. As they lowered themselves down a stack pipe one said: 'I feel like a commando.' The other replied: 'So do I – but where are we going to find any this time of night?'

That is more or less the same story – misinterpretation of sexual desire at a bizarre moment. But that version would not have offended the community half as much as that stupid four letter word. While I admire the mayoress's desire to avoid the usual starchiness of civic dinners, she should not try to pull her chain of office.

After all, who would ask her to speak again? 'Keep it clean' is a safe maxim for all public speakers, especially those whose personalities are not capable of getting away with the ingenious 'daring' of really professional comedians.

Refurbishing 'Unsuitable' Stories

Often we hear very funny – and witty – 'blue' stories which we feel, with a bit of a 'twist' we can clean up. This is possible providing we are not obvious about it. The surplanting of a passionate kiss for the act of copulation, however, never works ... it is always blatantly transparent to an audience! No, you are best advised to leave 'blue' jokes for their own little private bar.

However, there are some stories that are not necessarily blue but contain some rather sensitive ingredient which could offend certain audiences. I make no apology for repeating a story I have previously published, but I have never found its equal as an example of how one can alter an offensive story into one completely acceptable – and funny – for speeches to any audience.

The original was really 'sick'. A man is told by the doctor that his wife is dying. He goes up to see her and she tells him not to worry. 'A sturdy chap like you,' she tells her husband, 'will want to marry again after I've gone. I shan't mind, only, there's one promise I want you to make. Don't let her wear my clothes.'

'Oh,' says the husband, 'they wouldn't fit her, love.'

That is a Yorkshire story and almost impossible to tell in mixed company. Ruthless and cruel, it may have a terrible ring of truth about it, but is unnecessarily vicious. Yet I knew that the pay-off had great possibilities. What I had to get rid of was that death scene. So I worked on it for weeks – and finally came up with this :

'A newly-married couple had just made their wills at a solicitor's office. Over lunch they were discussing their future and the serious young husband said : 'If anything should happen to me, I shan't mind you marrying again – only don't let him wear my clothes . . .' And *she* replied : 'They wouldn't fit him, love.'

Note – I reversed the male and female roles, thus ensuring the ladies win. But if I recount it on a stag night, I change them back. But the death angle has gone, it is now a domestic story fit for any audience. I have even surplanted the clothing angle with more specialised apparel, cricket togs, evening tails for formation dancing, leather 'ton-up' gear, even golf clubs . . . 'Don't let him use my clubs, dear?' 'They'd be no good, he's left-handed.'

Another example. 'A woman sees an ambulance leave the house next door one Sunday morning. She rushes in to her neighbour and asks what has happened.

'It's me husband,' says the housewife. 'I asked him to go into the garden and cut me a cauliflower for lunch. He tripped on the step and broke his leg.'

'Goodness,' cries the neighbour, 'What are you going to do?'

'Open a tin of peas . . .'

Yet, in the original version I heard, the husband had died of a heart attack ! No audience wants reminding of that fate.

The same maxim applies to jokes about peoples of different skin pigmentation to your own. Any jokes which relies, for its laugh, on colour prejudice is a stupid risk to take in public speaking. For my part, I do use stories involving those from other lands living amongst us now. It is topical to do so, but I always avoid bias of religion, status or ignorance.

My favourite in this category is of a Yorkshire mill-owner standing glumly watching his premises burning fiercely. A small fireman beside him is playing a hose feverishly on the blaze.

'Where are you from?' asks the mill-owner.

'I am from Karachi,' says the fireman with a bright smile.

'Heck, you've been quick ... they're not here from Leeds yet ...'

There is no offence possible in that story, yet it does use an up-to-date community situation.

So check all stories you collect carefully. If there is half a chance of their offending, analyse them and see where you can alter the context, even to making it suitable for even just one particular occasion. It is a most interesting exercise for the imagination to say to yourself: 'Here is a gag with a dangerous element in it. Yet the over-all idea is funny. How can I eradicate that – yet still keep the laugh at the end?' Even with perfectly clean and all-purpose stories, you can still alter them round to suit your particular needs. They do not have to be blue or sick in the first place.

But it is no good reassuring yourself that you are broad-minded and that the audience must follow your lead. No audience will tacitly accept standards they themselves do not consider fitting for the occasion. If you wish to succeed you must please them as they *wish* to be pleased – or do not try to be funny in public. You have no alternative as they donate the applause and you, as an unknown, do not have a star comedian's reputation which sometimes sways an audience to accept blue material. But you can bet your boots, if it is in a speech, there will be some who object to it.

So aim to amuse, not shock. Believe me, to possess a reputation for being a reliable speaker can do you nothing but good in both your social and business world. But be insensitive to the susceptibilities of audiences and you will be the loser in many more ways than you think.

Laughter in General
Laughter is a real asset to keeping fit. I'm not kidding, it is.

It relieves tensions, you can 'let yourself go', and the muscular exercise also does you a power of good. The energy of laughter in the blood stream envigorates you, the heart and lungs are toned up and, say experts, helps the diaphram. It can also ease away unwanted fat! They use to say 'laugh and grow fat' but perhaps our happy, laughing scientists have proved otherwise.

But, above all, good natured laughter is the best social exchange in the world. American university students now take organised courses in it, a French psychologist teaches laughter as a prolonger of life, feeding it to students on record – perhaps using that gloriously absurd laughing policeman disc so popular in Britain in the 'thirties. However, our serious minded, latter-day generations say that 'laughter is only a fun thing', as if it is an emotion not to be equated with normal living. To me that is sadly limited thinking.

Pompous, self-assured people do not possess a sense of humour. Neither do self-styled revolutionaries. They see no purpose in it simply because they associate it with a happiness, and a freedom which is beyond them. They have a subconscious desire not to see any joke which has a bearing on their own environment or is likely to topple their own so-serious image. If they laugh at all, which is rare, it is only in triumph. The world takes itself far too earnestly in its dialogue and the chap who insists that he can 'see the funny side', rarely can. He sees only his side. It is only funny if he has made the joke. If it is against him, he is mortally affronted and insulted – the disease of egotism.

A true sense of humour needs a respectable I.Q., for you require both intelligence and humility in your make-up. Laughter is a spontaneous emotion and catches, in its reaction, completely unaware. That is its delight, the surprise element, the sudden 'good time' feeling. Laughter is not losing face, it is improving it. Ye now, so much has it declined that educational training courses have to be provided to keep it alive, as if it was a science available only to an élite. If it has become that, we have only ourselves to blame. We certainly shall not want study courses on how to cry!

Certain psychiatrists today have said that much of the mental illnesses and neuroses are caused by a dearth of the good, old-fashioned community belly laughs, the head thrown back, enjoying the beautiful helplessnesses of genuine, spirited laughter.

So, if you can use humour in your public speaking, do your best. You may help somebody.

Summary of HUMOUR IN SPEECHES

1. Study the suitability of stories for each speaking occasion carefully and re-hash the danger points liable to offend.
2. Speak within your orbit. Make your fun part of your personality and weave into your speech – not isolate it in patchwork parts.
3. Remember that, even with humour, you are still making a speech – not doing an 'act'.
4. Aim to please the majority of your audience, not a 'snide' minority of mates.
5. Keep alert for, and collate, the sayings you hear in your daily round. Check the press and magazines for apt anecdotes.
6. Do not tell stories 'off-the-cuff', rehearse them as thoroughly as the rest of your speech.
7. Never use the dialects to which you are unaccustomed.
8. Aim to amuse – not shock.
9. And, with any joke – if in doubt, leave it out.

CHAPTER SEVEN

Speakers on Their Feet

As I mentioned earlier in a different context, an audience sums you up visually as you rise, your subject temporarily forgotten for a few vital seconds. So appearance is important. The days of full evening dress are rare occasions now and, while a man may look his best in white tie and tails, those collars were hell to speak in. But, whether formal or not, a man should wear a collar rather too large than too small. The heat of the average dining room could well cause a swelling or a tightening here and there.

This applies equally to ladies. If you are wearing a new gown when you make a speech, do, I beseech you, rehearse in it first. Go right through the motions of rising, making the speech and sitting down again. Many a charming speaker has been hampered by loose shoulder straps and has to keep fidgeting while all the leering males are hoping for a revealing accident. Changes of temperature in rooms can alter fittings. What, in the dressmaker's, was a svelt line can become too tight or too loose in the heat of a crowded room. So when you select your evening wear, break it in gently, get to know the feel of it. Avoid long draping sleeves which can lasso a microphone or knock spectacles from the nose of those listening beside you. Too frilly a bosom can mask the notes on the table below you. Leave your arms free. Three-quarter length sleeves are best, minus jingling bangles that 'cymbalise' your every gesture. You may be sure, too, that if your girdle is going to kill you, it will begin its agony during a speech.

The nerves and tension of public speaking can play havoc with our comfort. A sweet lady once said to me : 'Every time

I stand up to speak, I feel eight months pregnant...' Yes, cumbersome and restricted, but as soon as she began to speak you would not think she had a nerve in her body. The woman speaker must avoid tight belts and aim for comfort before slimmed artificial waistlines. You ladies have to strike a happy medium between the too severe and the over-fussy in your apparel.

For men, too, long jacket or shirt cuffs can be irritating, having to be shot back at intervals. New shoes for both sexes may seem a strange speaking handicap, but to remain still on your feet is sheer agony if footwear pinches or, with ladies, the heels are too high so that you have to lean back to maintain an upright stance and so strain the calf muscles. And you men, if your trousers are too tight, you can never look relaxed. They may fit round the waist before you leave home – but after that dinner, you long to undo the top. So break-in and dress-rehearse in any new clothes you intend wearing for speech making.

Using a Microphone

Some speaking venues need them, others do not. A gathering of thirty to forty people should not require amplification for speeches – but it is surprising how many organisers will even lay on sound equipment in very small rooms for the most intimate occasions. However, I would rather they took that uneconomical step than fail to provide it for a vast hall with some five hundred people in it. Yes, I have suffered that horror – working in the centre of a ballroom at a buffet lunch without a mike, making a speech with the audience north, south, east and west of me. One had to shout simply because one could not actually face all of them all the time. Nuances had to go by the board as I competed with plate-rattling and glasses clinking.

As you progress in the speaking world you will find microphones are like cars; there are smooth, efficient ones and old bangers! Some are perfect for reception but the stand is tottery; others are at perfect height but behave like angry wasps at the receiving end. A microphone often starts the evening in excellent health but, by the time the toastmaster has moved it from speaker to speaker, it develops hiccups and burps. They are

155

delicate instruments and too often get some pretty rough handling in the course of a function.

Organisers do not, in my experience, pay sufficient attention to microphones and rarely have a qualified man on the spot to check the sudden whistles and wheezes. Much better, if only one microphone is available, to have it static on a rostrum or one set position in the room and ask all speakers to move to it, rather than keep jamming it down in front of them all over the room, the lead becoming entangled with surrounding ankles and chairlegs.

Organisers often expect a speaker to hand-hold the microphone without a stand. This is an unfair hazard. It restricts holding notes or making gestures. Few speakers have the pop-singer technique of gripping the trailing lead and often their voices fade as they forget to use it as a drinking glass. The hand mike is all right for memorised speeches or off-the-cuff compère announcements, but really, to be fair to a public speaker, the microphone should be on a stand and have a wide range of direction.

When you attend a function as a speaker, I advise that you take time out before it starts to check the microphone yourself. Slip into the room and study the scene before the audience gets in, so that you know in advance just what facilities you have on hand so that, if you have to improvise, you plan it with plenty of time before you rise to your feet. Have a word with any technician in charge. Are there any switches on the microphone which you must work yourself? This is especially important if, through sudden oscillation, you need to switch it off during your talk. And if the sound does let you down, stop and let it be adjusted. Do not press on without it, as I have seen, so that the audience, once attuned to the amplified voice, find your suddenly unaided tones thin in comparison. You are then in great danger of losing impact.

Nor do I think you should spurn the microphone as many veteran speakers do. 'I don't need it,' they boom in a smug way. But, if every other speaker uses it, such loners lose out. The timbre differs and today audiences are so used to radio and television that the amplified voice is acceptable. It also aids repose and projection. You can obtain subtle inflections with a microphone that would be impossible if the natural voice had to be lifted across a great hall. Mostly speakers who scorn to use a microphone are, if the secret were known, really afraid of it. They view it with apprehension and talk at it as if it was a snake rearing from an Indian charmer's basket.

Try and avoid clutching the microphone round the stem when speaking. This tends to bring you too close to it and create a chinese gong effect if you inadvertently touch the head. Check before you start speaking just how far you need to be from it. If you have no chance before the function starts, watch those using it before you, the toastmaster or chairman, and see how far they stand back from it. Check, too, that the mike does not hide your face. Adjust the height of the stem so that it is below your chin and that the audience can see your features clearly – especially your eyes. Some of those large-headed microphones can make you look like a martian in a collar and tie if your face is obscured.

A good microphone can be below the chin and tilted up to take your full range of voice. Some old-fashioned thistle types need to be under the lower lip to pick you up fully but, whatever the handicaps, let the audience see your eyes! Much depends on the sensitivity of the mike, but you must watch that you do not wheel around in your endeavour to take in all parts of the room. A good speaker should try and embrace all corners during his speech but, if your mike range is limited, remember that an audience must primarily hear you; seeing you is a secondary consideration in such circumstances. Nothing is more irritating than a head wobbling type of speaker who keeps losing the microphone every time he turns right and left, or nods up and down. All you hear is: 'It gives me great . . . some years ago . . . and your chairman said . . . as we all agree . . . a strange circumstance . . . who was a friend . . .' I call this a lighthousekeeper's speech for it sounds as if he learned it while the light kept coming round, going on and off in short bursts! However, a microphone is no excuse for lack of effort in voice projection; it magnifies a bad speaker, it does not improve him. I have heard a speaker much too close so that a hunter watch ticking away in his waistcoat pocket sounded just as if he was being eaten away by a death watch beetle. After twenty dreary minutes we wished he was! That watch should have been out on the table in front of him to remind him that he was well over his allotted time.

Microphones, like the speakers themselves, are temperamental things, useful only if treated delicately and with understanding. If you are unsure of them at a function, do not be too proud to ask for instruction from the expert on hand and leave the pre-dinner drinks to test them for yourself. Better than having to make blundering adjustments *after* you begin to speak. The general tendency is to speak too close to a microphone so that every breath sounds like an incoming tide. Keep the head back and let the audience see you possess a neck.

Rising to Speak.

First listen to the toastmaster or chairman announcing you, just to make sure he has his facts right about you. If he has not and the errors or omissions affect your subject, tactfully clarify after you have opened your speech with the necessary formal address. 'Ladies and gentlemen, your chairman has told you I am a schoolmaster . . . actually I am an education inspector . . .' Be sure the audience knows exactly who you are, or else you might find your speech going astray through no fault of your own. So always listen to your own announcement very intently.

When on your feet allow the room to settle. Do not, as has already been mentioned, rush into the speech. Let the applause die down while you adjust your cue cards below the microphone; smile if you feel like it, and then make your opening statement. 'Mr Chairman' (glance at him briefly, then out front again) 'ladies and gentlemen . . .'

Stance and Demeanour

Stand in a comfortable position, hands at your side. Not in pockets, jingling your key ring or loose change. Never put your hands in pockets, please; it does not indicate a relaxed appearance, as many think, but rather an off-hand approach. Keep the chest open and shoulders square, do not hunch up so that breathing is restricted.

The legs must be relaxed, slightly apart, the balance sustained slightly forward on the soles of the feet. Rock too far back on your heels and you can develop cramp. Aim to use the balls of the feet rather than the heels, but do not sway about. Take root first, then stand still, but loosely. Remain ramrod stiff and the calf muscles will soon begin to ache. The normal nervous stomach tensions before you speak can be easily transferred to the legs if you are not relaxed. Many a speaker will confirm that, if he or she has been a guest of honour and had to make a long speech, by the time they sit down they feel as if they had run a marathon so physically tired do they feel.

Anyone who has served on the forces will remember the orders . . . 'Attention, stand at ease, stand easy.' It is the middle one – 'Stand at ease' – you have to adopt when on your feet in public. One does not want to be altogether immobile. There are the starers, those who rise to speak and fix their eyes on the opposite wall and remain glued there for the whole discourse. Such speakers cannot make much impact. Then there is the type who fixes his or her eyes upon one member of the audience and appears to address the whole speech to him. The victim usually rises in a hurry after a few moments and slips out, sweating profusely, wondering why the speaker picked on him.

And there is the head waggler. He remains still in body, but his head rocks like a Punch and Judy puppet. This is often to be seen, sadly, on television screens . . . the speaker who cannot say anything without nodding. Would-be comic speakers are apt to seek extra emphasis this way, too, but it is ugly and amateurish. Watch any TV interview and you will be bound to see someone whose perky self-image makes them incline their head when listening to the question, to simulate 'listening', study their finger nails and even sit clasping their knees like a bohemian in Toulouse Lautrec's day. They would not do it at home, but they are trying too hard to give a performance of being at ease – hence their demeanour looks contrived throughout. What we do at close quarters in every day life may not be so important, but when we stand up in public for all to see, some mannerisms will prove a handicap in achieving a one hundred per cent concentration from your audience.

One day when we can not only hear our voices on tape but see ourselves on film cassette form, we will get a shock. And when, instead of showing round the family albums of 'still' photographs, we can be projected on the wall for all our descendants to see 'in action', we might well hide our heads in shame at our lack of repose. 'Why,' we will mutter, 'did I keep straightening my tie . . . ?'

But, maintaining the camera analogy, you as a speaker on your feet must cover the room, you have to 'pan' left and right and take in all the audience. Not in jerks, but in steady movements, always giving your full face to some part of the room. Naturally if the microphone is restricting, then those directly opposite will see more of your face than those on the periphery of the room, but at least sometimes attempt to work outside to the wings.

Rehearse standing up, too. You would be surprised how many word-perfect speakers have only practiced their lines sitting down! Suddenly on the night they find stance a problem. So you must find your ease at rehearsal. And if you wish to change stance slightly and transfer the weight from one leg to the other, do so during a pause, not in mid-sentence. Otherwise, when using a microphone you may waft away from it.

Using the Hands

Professor Bronowski, whose series 'The Ascent of Man' was in my layman opinion one of the great pieces of television education, used his hands almost all the time he spoke. His Jewish background may account for it, but never has an erudite man used fingers, palms and wrists more convincingly to convey his words. 'In vision' his every gesture was telling and effective.

But not all of us are so gifted – and, if the secret was known, I don't suppose that clever man realised just how much he did use his hands. Certain countries are more demonstrative than others. Italians and French are excitable and their hands thresh even if discussing a funeral. Indians and Pakistanis also like gesture . . . indeed the namaste greeting is one of the most beautiful in the world. I have seen an Indian girl student rise to speak in public and press her hands together under her chin, palm to palm, finger tip to finger tip – and smile. She made a splendid speech, but so beautiful was her repose that, even if she had talked nonsense, we would have forgiven her!

Ladies, nervous of their hands, are inclined to pick at the rings on their fingers, flutter their notes, twist a handkerchief or table napkin, or clasp and unclasp their hands as if miming 'anguish'. Men put their hands behind their backs, cup elbows, pluck moustaches, prod ears, fold arms, grasp lapels, or hook thumbs in waistcoats or tops of trousers! The art is to let your hands hang loosely at your sides and forget them. If you are holding notes with both hands (which is inclined to restrict good chest expansion), at least pause when you consult them and raise your head again before resuming your speech. Do not talk down into your notes or the microphone may not pick up your voice from that angle.

One chap I knew found his hands an embarrassment and so I advised him to stand *behind* his chair at dinners. When he rose to speak he would slip behind his chair and rest his hands on the top rail of the back. Prior to that he had always tried to rest his hands on the table below. Being a tall chap he thus spoke in a crouched position as if waiting for the starter's gun on a Marathon. But there came a time when he had to speak from the body of a hall, with no table in front and no chair back to take the strain. So engrossed was he in his speech that he failed to notice its absence. He spoke, arms held loosely at his side, simply because he did not think about them any more.

Being completely *au fait* with your subject will help you relax sufficiently to forget your hands. You don't think about them in ordinary life; why should you when you rise to speak? But you do . . . you become super-sensitive about them. The cure lies in being so completely absorbed and confident in what you have to say that you eventually forget your arms.

What you must not do is keep changing your arm position so that you appear to be impersonating an eight-armed eastern god. Keep as still as you can and only use your hands in definite, natural reactions.

Gestures in Speeches

Gestures must not be confused with gesticulation. Gesticulation is uncontrolled, an impulse of irritation, usually meaningless when equated with the spoken word. Gesture in a speech must add definite emphasis to your words. The spreading of hands to qualify a query, the shoulder shrug to indicate either bewilderment or acceptance of the inevitable, even a salute in a service anecdote or thumbs up sign are admissible in the right context. These 'actor' gestures often help the picture you are creating for your audience. But, in the main, keep your repose;

certainly do not windmill about. Raise your glass if relating a bibulous story, look at your watch to denote a time factor, fold your arms to impersonate a forbidding character in a joke – but do not ever, however incensed you may feel, bang your fist on your palm! Any speaker who works himself into a fenzy of blazing eyes and twitching nostrils, especially in a political speech, is guilty of 'hamming it up'. It rarely helps the cause, because it is so obviously bogus. No progressive idea can be imparted in a white-hot rage.

Gesture, beyond your natural habit, has therefore to be closely watched. Too often a speaker overplays it with pantomime double-takes and jerking the head back in mock horror. If they come naturally in rehearsal, modified gestures will look well but, if they are not spontaneous and are applied like a numbered drill exercise, they will not fuse with your words. They will be jerky, contrived and you will look like a mechanical toy.

Use of the Eyes when Speaking

Your eyes must reflect the mood of your words whether grave or gay. Some speakers' pupils do not match their dialogue. The material may be interesting, even amusing, but the speaker's eyes betray either anxiety or an almost blank disavowal of the utterance! But if your mind is fully on the job and prepared by rehearsal, your eyes should play their natural part.

For example, if you are pulling an audience's leg gently with some mock serious statement which you will eventually disclaim, your eyes will signify your true intention, for they counterbalance the words. And, if you are quoting some stupid statement made by a character in an anecdote, your eyes can roll upwards in despair at it, and be accompanied by a despairing head shake.

But, above all, never let your eyes appear furtive, darting round the room as if looking for a quick getaway. Some speakers seem to open their eyes wider when speaking publicly than in normal life, so that they give the appearance of being constantly scared. Perhaps they are – but they must not show it!

As one gains experience one can speak almost without actually seeing the audience at all. Your eyes work in conjunction with the scenes your speech is creating in your mind, smiling in conjunction with your mouth, or becoming stony if the mouth tightens. In new speakers one sometimes sees a gleek of a smile, but the eyes remain gimlet hard with nerves throughout.

It is all a question of rehearsal, so that your thought process is not divided between trying to remember the lines and creating an atmosphere of repose.

Spectacles

When normally worn by the speaker, of course, no trouble. But to those of us who need them for reading, then wearing them in public so that we can see our notes or cue cards can make us fidget with them. I do a lot of compèring, which means that I am handed information at the last minute, so I am obliged to wear reading glasses to see the names of prize-winners, raffle tickets and other 'surprise' items during a social evening. But I don't feel at ease with my glasses on my crooked nose, so, with a speech, I use much larger cue cards with the lettering thick and bold.

Speakers unused to glasses but needing them for notes are apt to push them over their eyebrows like Edwardian motorists, snatch them off to make points and, when running out of memory, jab the sidepieces in their ears in a hurried attempt to see their cue cards again. Ladies are more fortunate and can carry lorgnettes – provided they keep the cord under control. May I advise you not to wear a necklace if you use lorgnettes, otherwise during a speech the two can become inextricably knotted!

The answer to the occasional spectacle wearer is to rehearse with them – and abandon them on the night if one feels sufficiently versed in the lines. Otherwise use big capital letters on your cue cards, for these do obviate the use of glasses far more than typed or normal handwritten notes.

The Final Moments of a Speech.

Do round off a speech. I repeat my earlier advice. Do not end abruptly and sit down leaving the room surprised that you have finished. I am all for brevity, but it must be tempered with the natural courtesies and thanks.

You have finished your speech and, perhaps, you have triumphed beyond your, highest hopes. The room roars with applause and you may feel tempted, as an actor, to take a 'bow', in effect, and stand savouring it. I can't blame you – but do sit down immediately you have said your piece. By all means slightly incline the head (not an imperious nod!) and smile in acknowledgment if the applause is sustained – but, once down, do not rise again.

When the speech is over don't slump as if in a ringside corner after a heavyweight battering, however much it may feel like that. Sit down briskly and purposefully – and smile. Avoid, as I have often seen, the grim visage some speakers assume as they sit, as much as to say, 'My God, I've made 'em think, I'm a force to reckon with.' Perhaps the audience are only being polite in their applause . . . the handclap of relief that at last that's over!

If you are really being acclaimed, however, you may wonder, in early days of public speaking, just how to contain yourself. You don't know quite where to put yourself amid the vociferous applause. It is a glorious, but uncertain moment. Take a sip of your drink first. That always settles you. But certainly do not ignore your audience by suddenly engaging your neighbour in earnest conversation to cover your embarrassment. That looks – and is – rude, as if you have already dismissed them like a teacher clearing up her books after a class. Only turn to a neighbour when the applause is receding into mere desultory handclaps from your most loyal supporters in the room.

Accepting applause is a pleasing experience, but sudden nerves come with success as well as failure and you can appear rather cocky. No, you must just sit through it, looking suitably modest. Any speaker who gives the impression he or she is used to applause, that it is a daily occurrence in their lives, will soon hear it abruptly subside. Look into your lap if you are really moved by the reception, for, I can assure you, in really high-spot moments of triumph, especially if unexpected, they can bring you near to tears of gratification. If, of course, you receive a standing ovation, just bask in it. And smile!

Summary of SPEAKERS ON THEIR FEET
1. Rehearse in any new clothing to be worn on the occasion.
2. Check microphones and distance needed to stand from it.
3. Let the audience see your eyes.
4. Listen closely to the announcement of your speech so that

you may correct any errors which may affect your theme.

5. Allow the room to settle before you start.
6. Stand at ease – not at attention or slouch.
7. Move your head to cover the audience at each side.
8. Do not confuse gesture with gesticulation. Use hands moderately.
9. Take care not to fidget with reading glasses.
10. Round your speech off tidily; do not sit down abruptly.

CHAPTER EIGHT

The Talk or Lecture

While you will begin your career in the 'Social' or 'Business' speech field you will, if you are really keen, gradually move into wider fields of speaking dates. A man may well start with school or university debates, move through his own professional or commercial circles, broadening his scope by club and social functions. Indeed, he might become a mason, when he will find speaking in that ritualistic world demands a good memory and strict adherence to tradition. A woman, after similar scholastic or career beginnings, may branch into Women's Institute or similar community fields, or may move in the educational world where speaking well in public is absolutely vital. A classroom is often a far tougher assignment than a political rally.

But, after gaining this type of experience, you might wish to move into the 'talk' world or 'lecture', although that term is considered by some to be old hat now. However, it still aptly describes the educational or, informed discourse. Perhaps 'lecture' sounds too dictatorial for modern thinking . . . so we now just 'talk' on subjects.

There is a great deal of difference between the 'talk' and the 'speech' at a public function. The talk aims to 'teach', while the speech is to 'inform', or, on less serious occasions, to 'entertain'. Their ingredients overlap, of course. A talk must be entertaining, but it does last longer than a speech – or should, although many public speakers so often cannot separate the two. There are some speakers who will even turn a proposal of marriage into a lecture!

The fact that you can make a good public speech does not necessarily mean that you can give a 'talk' in exactly the same vein. The techniques are different. Speech-makers can adapt a subject, even when he or she has only a working knowledge of it, even confessing such shortcomings to their audience, but still be able to convey some valuable aspect of it. If the subject is, for example, construction of new roads, the speaker may not understand macadamisation or surface stresses, but he can be an authority on community living and homes on the edge of motorways. But, when lecturing, every aspect of the subject should be known . . . you must be an expert. If not, you may well find yourself at a loss during the question time which inevitably follows your talk. So, if you want to enter the 'talks' tour and go round societies, institutes and luncheon clubs, you must be A.1 in your subject. Your audiences seek, in the main, culture, not necessarily in a snobbish one-upmanship way but from a sincere desire to widen their knowledge.

But the 'talk' is not for the faint-hearted. It is a tortuous profession indeed, for you can, if mentally equipped, be paid for it. Authors, actors, painters, craftsmen, cooks, antique collectors, gourmets, Toms, Dicks and Harriets all deliver 'talks' on their pet subjects up and down the country the year round. Sometimes they are given at luncheon clubs, mainly to all-women audiences, others in civic or town halls supported by films, slides and other visual aids.

You cannot start lecture touring unless you are already sure you can speak well in public first, so there is no point in re-stressing the need for clear diction, a good vocabulary or use of microphones all over again. Yet some self-appointed lecturers still lack the rudiments, I'm afraid, still mumble, blather and seem uncertain of the words they must have said a hundred times before. They assume because they are experts on their subject that they need not rehearse. They may have the finest story to tell in the world, but many still make it about as interesting as the Repeal of the Corn Laws would be to an audience of unmarried mothers. With lecturing sheer weight of subject is insufficient. You need a strong personality to get it across – and to be able to answer convincingly off-the-cuff questions at the end.

Mostly the audiences for such 'talks' are educational establishments, society and distaff luncheon clubs. I can assure my fellow men that an audience of some two hundred women in their best hats is a pretty – but formidable – sight when you, the only male, rise to address them. But you, yourself, do not present any such novelty at that moment, for you are only one of some fifty speakers of both sexes they will hear during the year. They have rules you must obey, they are not averse to wit, but they do not want to laugh all the time. But certainly they are quick to note the imposter. Dear old Jollyboy who loves the ladies, God bless 'em, with his rose in his buttonhole and his talk on some extraordinary hobby suddenly finds them cold and impersonal. The more roguish he becomes, the less impact he will have. The ladies are saying within themselves 'God help his wife!' or 'I wouldn't give that old fraud house-room'.

All-women audiences like dignity, so any impudence must be tempered by good taste. Certainly the irrelevant risqué story is right out. They are the employers, you are the lone worker in their pay. And woe betide the committee if you fall short of their high standard. They will complain to the agents booking you or to you, yourself, if they feel you fall short of professional standard. And also tell other societies contemplating engaging you!

For ladies embarking on a 'talks' career, there are similar hardships in facing your own sex. Your appearance will be under scrutiny, your frock, hat and jewellery will be noted with penetrating eyes. I am not being particularly critical of all-women clubs; it is just that they provide the majority of audiences in this field. And, as they are paying you, are entitled to call the tune. They want a cultural talk on an intelligent subject delivered professionally. In the same way as a sensible housewife shops wisely so will she view the many speakers her club subscription helps to pay for every week. Thus – if speakers want their money, they must provide the right goods. Far from condemning them, I applaud this frank, logical attitude. They have no time for the second-rater.

If ever you attend, as I have done, a speaker's agency lunch when all the chairwomen and secretaries foregather in a London hotel to meet personally the available speakers for the new season, you will appreciate the ordeal, however sensible it is. With badges on lapels or frocks which states our names and speaking subject we are surveyed by these highly responsible ladies. Some, because they do not like wearing reading glasses in public peer at your badge an inch from your nose. They check your details in the brochure they carry and discuss with you the possibility of your speaking for them in their home town. They make surreptitious notes – how we'd love to see what they've written!

So the good 'speaker' with an interesting subject can earn a minor living in this field. And we are deeply grateful to these all-lady institutes who book us. At least they do expect to pay us – their male counterparts mostly expect we will do it for nothing!

That is, of course, partly the reason why one hears so many poor speeches at functions organised by masculine clubs when the speaker is asked 'for free'. By the very payment of a fee the ladies ensure their speakers have a contractual bond to be well-versed and well-rehearsed in their subjects. And of course no speaker at a ladies' luncheon club is ever drunk . . .

When going in for lecturing in any form, you must be prepared for the loneliness of the long-distance speaker. At after dinner engagements there is always a session with the organisers after your stint, a nightcap with the other guests before bed in the hotel. But with luncheon talks there is a much tighter time schedule. You do your job, reply to questions and acknowledge the vote of thanks. Then, half way through the afternoon you are on your way, by train or car. It can be very taxing, as many busy speaking personalities have found, cramming lunchtime work in with their evening activities. So, for your health's sake, do not, even when experienced, take on too much. The lolly may be tempting, but can the heart stand it? Such arduous speaking sessions, day after day, have been the cause of health breakdowns among some very famous people. The nerve strain may not be apparent even to the speakers themselves – but it can take its toll. In any case you will not enter this field until you have a lot of general public speaking experience first.

Treatment of 'Talks'
Often speakers, although expert in their particular subjects, do not assess correctly their different audiences. They give the same talk regardless of who is seated before them. You must apply the horses for courses adage here.

If you are talking about banking, insurance, even our old jack of all trades, ZENZ, you must still analyse the best approach to each *particular* audience. Addressing school-leavers you would emphasize, above all other aspects, the value of ZENZ as a future career rather than as a product. But if an all-women's audience, then you play down the career side and elevate ZENZ in a practical, domestic point of view. And, if your audience is a general one in a public hall, you must cover all aspects, employment, practical value, costs, ingredients – in fact everything that goes to make up ZENZ.

But beyond the commercial 'selling' fields, there are speakers in the various art forms. If an author or actor is facing a student group, then they will want to know the practical ways of becoming writers or performers, as well as attitudes to public demand. But if a women's institute or public hall audience, then those who have ambitions in those fields have already either achieved professionalism or remained mere interested amateurs and so the speaker's best tactic is anecdotal, giving examples of other people's success or failure amid the hazards and bouquets of that particular career. For an author to try and instruct a middle-aged audience how to become a professional writer is unlikely to be of much practical value to them. Anyone who has had the real flair – and not just imagined he has – either already knows the ropes or has abandoned the project years ago. The same also applies to most creative ventures.

You cannot make painters, writers, actors, hairdressers, conjurors, tailors or what have you out of mature people especially if it has not already occurred to them to try. So you alter the approach from the instructional to the *reviewing* of an occupation. One can, of course, strike a balance in subjects like needlework or cookery, when quite a few in a women's club audience would be already versed in one form of it. Then they can be taught to adapt the skill they already possess to another but, to them, new alternative form.

Audiences like to be educated – but not 'taught'! They enjoy absorbing culture in a take-it-or leave-it manner, applying your data freely to their minds without it being forced on them as a dogma. Never assume for one moment that everyone in the room, whether student, club member or general public, is agog for your knowledge. Always assume that their interest is only mild, and that your job is to try and increase that fragmentary attention to deep interest. Many a speaker comes away unexpectedly pleased that his talk has commanded some highly intelligent questions at the end. But, if he has strode on that platform so over-confident that he will cause headlines in the local newspaper, he will be deeply disappointed.

Question-time after Talks
The usual routine is for the chairman to ask the audience for questions after you have completed your talk. And, from these, you can ascertain just how well your talk has gone. Sometimes the questions reveal a singular lack of appreciation. Question time is the acid test. If you have waffled off the subject, have become caught up in some long explanation of something madam chairman has said in introducing you, you may well fall short of expectations.

But if the questions are relevant, challenging and provided you *do* know the answers, you have made real impact.

Mark you, some questioners rise up merely to try and floor you! They are the 'I'm-as-good-as-you-are' pragmatists . . . they only question you so that their own voice can be heard. The ego 'I' begins their question . . . 'I cannot agree that . . .' or 'I dispute your fact that' . . . to criticise you for criticism's sake in a sense of rivalry. But you still have to treat them politely . . .

The question you must most beware of is the smiling, polite one. 'You said so-and-so . . . but is it not a fact that . . . ?' and then, 'squelch', you are toppled by an irrefutable fact quite unknown to you. Oh boy, it's a dull-thudding moment. That is why, when you prepare your talks, you must have your facts right – and any that may seem off-centre must be qualified by you during your talk, and not be left as bait with which you can be hooked at question time. If one item is wrong in your talk, the audience will question the authenticity of the rest.

If their subject does not obviously invite much response at question time, some speakers are quite clever at stimulating it. They rise themselves and ask the audience questions – 'Did any lady here feel that . . . ?', or 'Are there any of you who thought, when I spoke of . . . ?', etc. There might be a general murmur and he proceeds to cover the points he has himself raised. That usually brings forth a few real queries from the audience. This is not sheer cunning, but a device to stir some rather shy audiences. If the speaker is, for example, a 'star', many members are perhaps nervous of addressing him or her, so they need just a little extra nudging.

Certain questions may seen pathetically irrelevant. As witness the old lady who, after hearing a local government speaker on traffic problems in her locality, posed a question concerning the danger of her cat being run over. The room sniggered with ugly intolerance. But the speaker did not join them. He first asked the lady's name and then answered her, skilfully using the cat – and its nine lives – as being synonymous with the danger to children playing in the street – and the peril of losing a loved one. Gradually the cat was forgotten, but the old lady's query had not only been treated courteously and effectively but advantageously to the speaker. If you can adopt that attitude on the community platform, showing real concern for the individual and successfully appraising their personal problems in the light of greater ones, you should be in the House of Commons, my friend . . . and not before time !

Making an Entrance
Everything I have said about stance, poise and appearance in speech making is applicable to instructional talks. But there is one additional requirement – a good walk. You will not, as a guest speaker, always be confined behind luncheon, dining or committee tables. You will undoubtedly have to work on big platforms and stages. You may have to enter from the wings, when introduced, and move to the centre. And audiences watch you very closely.

It is useless to regard that entrance as unimportant, reassuring yourself that they have come to hear you, not see you. As we know, they start their summing up of your style from the time they first see you, not hear you . . . and unlike the banqueting room speech, you have a much longer interval of silence as you reach the lectern, table or, in many cases, nothing at all but a bare stage with not even a chair in sight. On the political or committee platform you will enter with other officials, but, when giving a personal talk, you often have to come on alone.

So, if that entrance is at all self-conscious, you are liable to make a studied appearance. You are so aware of being watched that your leg muscles stiffen, you look stilted and your demeanour is contrived. You strut or march to centre stage. As first impressions with an audience are very important, to appear either too confident or sidle on as if trying to get lost in the back curtains puts the audience on edge.

Some speakers well used to public appearances and giving the same talk week after week, saunter on with an aloof expression, giving an impression of boredom. And they find to their cost that their familiarity does breed contempt. Others, the more absent-minded academics, their hair and clothes in disarray, blunder on as if needing a compass or map reference to reach their focal point. Then they bob and weave about, peering at the audience as if surprised to see them. And I have seen two blasé speakers casually stub out a cigarette in centre stage before opening their lecture! Some slummuck across the stage so slowly, appearing to hope an earthquake will cause the speech to be cancelled, while others dart across like a sprinter and even start speaking before they have reached their lectern or table.

The best guide to achieve a good stage entrance and walk is to imagine you are a guest arriving at a party. You don't know the other guests well yet, but the hospitality is good and you are determined to enjoy yourself. You look eager and alert, and walk easily but purposefully to the centre of the platform.

Give an audience time to look at you, however nervous or anxious you are to get on with it. Make sure you have silence when you begin; do not talk into the welcoming applause. That is merely a nice formality – prior to assessing your ability – a form of encouragement. But it is the applause at the end which counts!

With lady speakers I stress again the value of slim line apparel. If you are working in stage lighting, keep your dress reasonably modest. If you appear too opulent with glittering ear-rings and necklaces which catch the lights, you can create a false impression out front. And some jealousy perhaps! Look smart, not wealthy! Anyway, always avoid long necklaces and those bangles which clink irritatingly when you raise your arms.

What the audience want to see is a reposed figure with perhaps a welcoming smile, who nods appreciatively to the applause with only a slight inclination of the head. You are not performing a stage role, so do not bow low or curtesy! Professional tricks like that can be off-putting to a 'talk' audience. Your entrance is not a take-over of the audience. You have come to instruct entertainingly; you want to create a quietly confident intimacy with the audience. Remember, you will never get to know them – but everyone out there will take home their own particular impression of you. It is a sobering thought.

Rehearsals for Talks
Absolutely essential. You must write out your lecture as you would a speech. It is a much longer task and timing the length is just as necessary. If the organisers want half, three-quarters or even a full hour, you must obey. And you must allow for questions at the end, so don't over-run and have them all piling out to catch buses and trains before the chairman rises to thank you. If it is a public hall with admission charges, you are more than ever obliged to keep to your brief. The audience want their money's worth and if you let them down they will stay away from succeeding speakers. It may be an unfair judgement, but such are the anomalies of public opinion.

Try out your lecture either on a group of friends or a local society willing to be guinea pigs. Offer it but make it clear you are new to the game and ask them to be candid about it afterwards. It will serve you well and avoid you making a lot of mistakes in the future.

It is not advisable to try out parts of a lecture in ordinary speeches. The techniques are different and you run the risk of an uneven presentation when you become more familiar with one section and under-rehearsed with another. The talk will lack fluency and become unbalanced.

Rehearse a talk in full, resorting to the cue card system eventually if you want to take notes on the stage. Do not carry on a thick wodge of notes. It is even more essential that you keep your head straight and look out over the audience. That should be your eyeline – about a foot over the heads of those in the stalls. If there is a balcony, work up to that, but don't get fixed on it. Let the head move easily.

Gradually you will so familiarise yourself with your talk that you can leave the cue cards in your pocket. But have them there in case you get a mental blockage. That happens, strangely enough, when you are at your most confident. And, at the end, make notes of the questions you were asked; you may not have been quite satisfied with your answers and need to rephrase them if they crop up again. And sometimes a good question causes you to rewrite a section of your talk to clarify the point for future audiences.

You cannot, of course, anticipate questions but, if a talk is well balanced, the same questions are often asked. Usually they are slightly off the main topic, but nevertheless important to certain people in the audience, when different minds get to work on your words each week. Use relevant anecdote freely to illustrate your points – but not jokes. Certainly if you can raise laughs, do so, but don't give talks solely with that intention. Only a few professionals can do that – and they have the head start of reputation! So gain that first . . .

'Talk' Titles and Avoiding Obscurities

All speakers must give their talks a self-explanatory title – 'Exploring the Sahara Desert' . . . 'Flower Arrangement' . . . 'Home Wine Making' . . . 'Infant Care' . . . 'Round the world in an Open Boat'. Other subjects may need some qualification on the billing. 'The Rodeos of America and Mexico' might be sub-titled 'The Horse Skill of Cowpunchers', in case 'rodeo' is not generally known. But a few amateur lecturers are apt to give their lecture an obtuse, vague title, as if they were writing a novel . . . 'Night of Lanterns' gives no real indication that it is a description of a Chinese festival, nor does 'Over the Hills and Far Away' tell an audience that you are speaking about the Pennines.

Titles are important and they must be as crystal clear as if on a poster to attract the customers. Any talk whose title has to be explained to a committee booking a speaker starts him or her off with a disadvantage. Societies like to know exactly what to expect in substance, even if the lecturer's style remains a mystery until he begins. So avoid gimmicky titles.

You must be sure when lecturing that you do not assume your audience already knows the rudiments of the subject. Much depends upon what it is, of course. With 'Infant Care' no explanations are necessary unless your audience is entirely teenagers and you are part of a special instructional course. But if you are 'Exploring the Sahara' you can begin with 'I went to the Sahara Desert which, as you all know, is in Africa . . . half of them, may not, but you pay them the compliment of a 'pretence assumption' to make sure every member of your audience is with you. You do not speak of *regs* and *ergs* without explaining that they are 'rocky plains' and 'seas of sand'. Too many lecturers get carried away like this. They give lectures on subjects like desert conditions suitable only for British Museum students already possessing background knowledge, rather than remember they are lecturing in Little Twitchington church hall on the Essex border in the parish of St Jude. They forget that ninety-nine per cent of every audience will have been no closer to such a subject as the Sahara than seeing a camel in a zoo.

Visual Aids at Lectures
Graphs, maps and charts are very useful at sales talks for small audiences who sit close to the speaker. But, if you are working in a public hall, do make sure everyone can see them clearly. Nothing is more annoying for an audience than when the front few seats can see something which the back rows cannot! It is useless to hold up a crocodile's tooth – but you can show a packed theatre an elephant tusk! Like a magician doing card tricks in the Albert Hall, you will not succeed if you have to ask your audience to take your word for it you are holding the Jack of Diamonds! Rather use no visual aids at all than too insignificant for all to see. A good idea is to put objects on display afterwards so that those interested can file up on the stage and inspect them as you explain them. You have to bear in mind the size of your hall when you propose using wall charts and working models. Mostly these are not much use in a room beyond the average-sized school classroom.

The inclusion of lantern slides and film make a lecture for me extremely interesting. It also gives the speaker and the audience a rest from the single voice. But lecturers who employ these added attractions must be prepared to be turned down by certain societies. The famous round-the-world yachtsman, Sir Alec Rose, was once rejected by a society as a speaker using films, because the ladies said quite emphatically they 'did not want to sit there in the dark' !

There are certain societies who dislike mechanical apparatus being rigged up in their halls or seeing some man in overalls playing about with plugs and erecting screens during the lunch before the speaker starts his lecture. Even if all is made ready *before* they sit down, it creates an air of surrounding untidiness some precise minds object to. They have every right to their opinion – although I must confess they miss some jolly fine talks because of this prejudice.

Always check very carefully any visual aids you need before you make your entrance. Idle hands may have moved something you have so carefully placed on stage. If you are using a film projectionist, go through the procedure with him carefully. Give him a good cue sheet so that he knows exactly when to run the film or change the slides. In the latter case you can use the old-fashioned clicker, but make sure he can hear it !

Do not embarrass any local willing helper by taking it for granted he knows what you want. Get with him an hour before-hand and go through every detail of change from voice to visual aid, what lighting you will require on stage and any extra props, e.g., a table for equipment which you wish to demonstrate or, if you are speaking on a darkened stage, that your lectern light is in working order. I have known that nuisance – down go the lights and I switch on a lone bulb – phut – nothing happens, and the whole place is in darkness. Then my querulous voice – 'Is an electrician in the house . . . ?' Now I test it before the audience take their seats.

Do not send the organisers a list of your wants without checking when you arrive, that they have all been provided – and understood. Most speakers bring their own accessories with them, but some ordinary available furniture props they do not need to carry. But they can be put in the wrong place if you do not check. Much might depend on whether you are right or left handed, for example . . . put a table the wrong side and an awkward change round has to be made.

There is only one way to obviate any of these hold-ups. Be early for your speaking dates. Rather arrive an hour too soon than rush in through the stage door at the last minute, panting and with no time to wash or set your platform to your liking. In theatres the rule for actors is that they must be in their dressing-rooms at least half an hour before curtain-up. Apply that rule to your speaking dates. When you are on a large public platform you need that professional touch of efficiency. We may be quite adept at getting out of speaking mishaps – but it is far better for the audience's concentration if they don't arise in the first place.

Summary of THE TALK OR LECTURE
1. Never try to start your career in this line. Get used to ordinary 'speech' audiences first.
2. You must be expert in your subject, completely expert.
3. Adjust your 'talks' to suit the various audiences – do not rely on giving the same approach each time. Some subjects need adjustment to different standpoints.
4. Dress unpretentiously and with as slim a line as possible.
5. Make notes of any questions posed to you after your talk so that, if particularly relevant, you can embody them in your talk for the future.
6. Make a good purposeful 'entrance'.
7. Rehearse all 'talks' thoroughly.
8. Give such 'Talks' self-explanatory titles, clear to all as to subject.
9. Avoid blinding with science.
10. Use discretion when presenting visual aids – take size of hall into account.
11. Always be early for any 'talk' so that you can check all necessary equipment.

CHAPTER NINE

A Miscellany of Speaking Hints

Over the years, touring around many parts of the world, I have
gathered together several little wrinkles which might help you
through the early days of speaking nerves while you are still
finding your feet. In public speaking you must make each facet
of it as comfortable as possible for yourself. So here are a few
random notes from an old horse from many a course . . .

A Speaker on the Road
Over the years I have learned how to equip myself when going
on speaking jaunts. One of the biggest miseries is a paperless
toilet! Town halls, railway stations, trains, community centres,
seedy hotels – someone has either pinched the toilet roll, or it is
a soggy mess on the floor. So I always carry sheets of it in my
wallet – even though occasionally I have had to apologise to
railway booking clerks for inadvertently proffering it as a
banknote! Ladies should carry tissues – far more hygienic than
some of the textures public conveniences offer.

Always keep a special fob pocket or, with ladies, a special
handbag compartment or purse, for small change. Hoard it for
days before your speaking stint, so that you have it readily
available for telephone boxes in strange towns when the car
sent to meet you is not there or you have lost your way. The
odd gratuity is always handy when a speaker wants some special
favour – even to snatching a quick cup of tea during a train
wait. Loose change is vital if you are pressed for time – or get
stranded. And, if in a strange town, always buy a copy of the
local evening paper. It might help your speech with some topical
reference.

Even if your speaking engagement does not involve you staying overnight away from home, always take hair brush, comb, clothes brush, spare handkerchiefs and soap and towel. It is surprising how often these are not available and you are forced to speak still feeling grimy from the journey. Pack them in the boot of your car or carry them in a hold-all. Even if not staying the night I always pack a toothbrush and paste as well. If you do get the chance to clean your teeth after a meal before you speak, it does freshen up the mouth.

At the earliest opportunity after your speech, check your cue cards and mark in any points you feel, with hindsight, need adjustment for future use. If some point has misfired or gone off like a damp squib, tick it for re-writing. Do it as soon as you can after speaking, otherwise, in the heat of the moment, it can be forgotten. If you are driving home, do it in the car park before you switch on the engine. On the train it fills up the journey time. If you are staying overnight after the engagement, study those cards before you go to bed while all is still fresh in your mind.

If you have received private hospitality, make sure you obtain the name and address of your host and hostess, so that you can personally acknowledge their kindness. Please do not, as some speakers do, take them for granted as part of the over-all organisation. Many clubs, to save hotel expenses, ask their members to put up visiting speakers on a sort of rota system. It is never easy for them, taking a complete stranger into their homes, so write the letter of thanks yourself.

Always acknowledge by letter any fees or expenses you may receive, unless booked by an agent who will do the paying out himself. As many functions today have to be financially self-supporting, honorary treasurers cannot wait for bank statements and cashed cheques before clearing up accounts.

You can save yourself considerable personal expense if you keep 'scrap' paper. I draft speeches on the back of advertisements, old calendars, electoral promises, unimportant correspondence . . . and over the years must have saved hundreds of pounds outlay on paper.

Of course, when you get into the professional speaking and lecturing field which may be supplementary to your ordinary income, use an accountant. There are certain expenses allowed, but it is as well to have them sorted out by an expert. Do not fail to return any such income. The venues at which you speak will make their own returns for tax purposes, so your name will catch up with the authorities eventually. And they are not likely to be so generous over travelling and other sundry allowances if you give the impression that you were attempting to bilk them! Many a speaker and entertainer I know has been bowled out by tax authorities, simply because his name was on a menu or his speech reported in a local paper!

By speaking in public it can be argued sometimes that you are promoting yourself either artistically or businesswise. Appearing on platforms may help you publicise in some way a personal project. An accountant can advise you on your claims for this sort of public speaking and argue it out for you.

Use of Intervals by Speakers

At dinners there is usually a break between coffee and the first speech. A speaker should excuse himself or herself before that interval is called so that he or she can avoid crowded toilets. In some venues with limited accommodation the speaker is often at the end of a long queue, not good for nerves or peace of mind. He has to rush back, hands still damp from soggy towels and apologise to the chairman looking round anxiously for him.

So go out *before* the general guests. Excuse yourself at coffee time and have the wash-room to yourself, when the towels are dry. I wash my face in cold water, damp the back of my neck if the dining room has been over-warm, adjust my tie and the few strands of hair left on my dome. I also brush lapels, shoulders and shirtfront in case ash has fallen on them, which at a distance can look like dandruff. Then, on my return to the room, when the chairman does call the 'natural' break and the room clears, I remain at the table comfortably studying my notes and inserting any last minute additions, or striking out anything not applicable.

At this stage you know what sort of audience you can reasonably hope for, so you can make final adjustments. Even if I am chairman, I always ask the secretary to take my place while I attend to my own needs *before* the specified interval. Then, if there is some panic on, at least I am available in the room and not caught up in a loo queue, yelling to someone who seems to be immersed in a good book, to 'hurry up in there'!

Ladies do not put such a strain on themselves as men do by eating a full meal washed down with five pints of bitter; they do not have this stampede. But, as with men, I advise that they, too, make themselves beautiful before the ordinary general interval, instead of trying to refurbish lipstick amid jostling arms. It also avoids any speaker hearing caustic remarks about themselves from well-wined guests who, having no idea who is at their elbows, anticipate that you will be dull and boring!

Audiences

They are not easy to assess! Indeed, what makes an audience enjoy your speech one night and, a week later, in another town, give it a tepid response, is one of the mysteries which must have first bothered touring stage players in the early 17th century. Actors know all too well the hazard of a play doing big business in one theatre and dying a death in another.

No one yet has ever come up with a solution to the mystery of why a crowd of entirely divergent characters get together under one roof to be entertained or informed and band themselves in one large mould of hilarity, apathy, boredom or hostility. Atmosphere has a lot to do with it, of course. If there is a general upset in the community beyond the hall doors where you are speaking, the anxiety felt by all the audience may reflect in the attention they give you as you speak. Outside influences play a large part, but sometimes they also occur within the room or hall. Noisy drinkers who unnecessarily heckle the speakers at a dinner can spoil it for the majority, while a poor meal, abysmally served, can wreck the best speeches in the world.

But never make the mistake of blaming an audience for your failure to impress them. You cannot put yourself above them – you cannot consider yourself the only one in step. You have to please them, not they satisfy you. But if you do give them what they want – then you will know very clearly you have succeeded – and adore that audience for being so discerning of your talent!

The excuse of a bad audience for failure is a confession that your personality did not fit. Sometimes it may not be your fault. Poor speakers preceding you might leave the audience as Shakespeare says in King John 'bethumped by words', that not even your expertise can lift them up again from the stupor into which they have been driven. Here you can only do your best without playing down, bullying or patronising them.

A more obvious audience assessment is possible if you, as I have done, have even spoken to or entertained either children or really old folk. If all is not crystal clear to them, both young and old audiences become easily distracted. Children, because their innate curiosity is dissatisfied or they cannot equate what they are seeing or hearing with some facet of themselves. Old folk, being also sometimes hard of hearing, must comprehend in simple terms and be kept on the track of the subject. Otherwise their minds are apt to wander off in a chain of personal recollections peculiar to themselves and far from the subject under discussion. They are past wanting to learn, bless them; they want only to be reminded.

Now these two childlike and old characteristics manifest themselves in lesser degrees in the average young to middle-aged audiences, in the 'what's in this for me' attitude I have mentioned earlier. However, being more discerning and alert for that practical purpose, they have the power to concentrate more fully.

But it is a sobering thought that far less people actually sit in audiences today than once they did. Theatres and cinemas are thinner on the ground now that more professional entertainment is engineered into the home. So, with a lessening experience of sitting beside strangers, audiences today are filled more by suspicion and apathy. Only the tavern bonhomie 'live' entertainment seems to rise above it. Certainly bingo halls are packed – but the objective is self-interest for every pencil-poised member and the laughter engendered by an engaging 'caller' is inflamed by the anticipation of winning.

Experienced speakers try to analyse audiences, assessing both mood and temperament, and speak accordingly. This is easier at a dinner where he or she can sit through other speakers' efforts first and watch points. A lecture needs more careful nursing in the early stages because you alone are the guinea pig for each particular audience. If your topic is serious and you sense the sound waves of restless levity out front, then you have to try and intersperse some light relief. Good speakers know they cannot dictate to an audience – but they can woo it! The egotist who assumes before he starts that an audience is already sitting at his feet, servile, adoring and ready to accept his every word, soon hears that grim undertone buzz of chat as he proceeds with his witless words. Such self-opinionated persons make poor speakers because they will not accept that others should hold opinions different from their own. So they are amazed – and disgusted – with audiences who apathetically fail to respond or openly heckle them.

Of course in past decades many old pontificators relied, perhaps subconsciously, on old world politeness and traditional manners to allow them to drone on minus criticism, which continually gave them a false sense of importance. But that tolerance is dying fast. Audiences, used to the professionalism and sometimes conversely, lower standard of television in their homes, are more volatile, more destructive. If they have paid for a ticket they feel they are entitled to voice disfavour if they have not received a high standard of performance.

You stand or fall by the reception your audiences give you ... so study them, these motley gatherings of individuals, and do your best for them.

Critics

As it is in the nature of man to be mean with congratulation and liberal with criticism, we must remember that our audiences do not even begin their estimation of our ability as we do! There are always characters in the audience who feel they can do better. Vanity, all is vanity – and there are a lot of jealousies in the speaking circuits. Some people just cannot support a general acclaim ... it goes against the grain to help another's success. So, by tearing your speech apart with acid, lone-voiced criticism in the bar after the function, they enjoy being the solitary decrying minority. And often envy and malice are masked by some high-flown but discordant opinion of your effort. It usually manifests itself in remarks like: 'Well, I thought that speaker terrible – but I supposed he was all right – if you like that sort of thing.' Damning with taint phrase!

These barbs often come from a local favourite who, for

once, finds himself put in the shade by a more experienced guest speaker. Instead of subscribing to the general enthusiasm, he must draw attention to his own ability by a censorious attitude. Mostly such critics show themselves up in their true colours – and their once staunch supporters see them as the frail wailers they really are.

Then there is the acknowledged academic-type speaker who suddenly finds himself up against a humorist who reduces the room to hysterics. The pundit hates him and sits listening to him with a pained expression. It doesn't fool anyone – he's just furious he is not top-dog that night. But there is the reverse of this coin – the blue comic who is followed by a quiet speaker who is so expert in a droll technique of comedy that the audiences roll about in delight at the sheer unexpectedness of the approach. Then the blue comic bites his nails and snarls: 'What's so funny about that . . . ?'.

Analyse the reason and you will find that the popular speaker has taken the trouble to please, not imperiously done his own thing. It is as simple as that – you cannot beat the ticket-buyers, so join 'em. And usually the solitary carping critics are on the top table and haven't paid for their tickets anyway.

But if someone is willing to give you sound criticism . . . not aloud in a room full of people, but quietly between yourselves, then listen. 'Forgive me, young man,' said a voice at my elbow once in my early days, 'I happen to be a barrister . . .' 'Tell me then,' I said mournfully, 'please tell me . . . what do I do wrong?' He did, kindly but candidly. I had started quietly, but changed my demeanour half way through the speech when I realised the audience were on my side. So I ended rather too importantly . . . and went on far too long. I had begun as my normal self, but, with a feeling of confidence, I began, in effect, to 'strut' and put on an act as I became conscious of un-expected success. I learned the lesson. A speaker, I know now, is only as good as the last sentence he or she utters . . . you have to maintain your standard. So listen to all criticism – for even a malevolent, biting one can touch on a useful point. Never lose your temper with critics, of course; if you have pleased the over-all audience there cannot be much wrong with your tactics, so sleep easy! A jealous critic won't!

Booking Speakers

The eternal problem of function organisers is finding speakers. There are plenty about but, outside the big cities, local talent is often over-used simply because it is difficult to bring in strangers from outside. Indeed, such a speaker invited by one organisation in a town often finds he has to do the rounds of all the main societies there, if he or she is successful, as their name is handed on as one who 'has tongue, will travel'.

After-dinner speakers are usually engaged by reputations being passed on. A guest hears a speaker in London and buttonholes him to see if he can travel to Manchester for another society. That is the way it happens. Your committee or selection board should be comprised of men and women who move around the social, political and commercial fields a good deal. But these good people must be reliable, in that they know the audiences for whom they are selecting speakers. Otherwise over-enthusiasm can lead to gaffes, such as the robust football club speaker being booked to address a gathering of astronomers just because one well-wined guest found him personally funny somewhere else and suggested him for a completely different function atmospherically. That is neither fair on the speaker nor the audience.

Speakers should be selected with care – by committee. If you allow your overworked secretary to engage them all, then they may well be all cast in the same mould, simply because the secretary has a personal preference for such speakers. Then the evening will lack variety and be as dull as taking eight national anthems for your Desert Island Discs.

So, if you need four speakers, to follow your chairman, you choose a strong one to follow your chairman's obviously experienced opening speech. Put your two less experienced (or local lads or lasses who are in their early stages) in the middle and end on your most humorous speaker who can, if necessary, lighten the load of the earlier and more weightier words of the pundits. Nothing unbalances an evening more than putting your most amusing speaker on too early. Brilliant speakers like Dr Dickson Wright, Humphrey Tilling, Clement Freud or David Frost would completely wreck following speakers if they did not close the bill. Yet organisers do stubbornly disregard this sometimes and speaker number two sits down to a storm of applause with three far less interesting speeches still left on the card. The old music hall performer's cock-crow of triumph always comes to mind on these occasions – when they left the stage to a rousing reception, they would say to the next act waiting grimly in the wings – 'Follow that!'

So balance your bill, book it in effect with a strong opening and closing speech – and always end on the light relief. Speakers on a bill should be complimentary to each – but not the same. Three speakers, say, a solicitor, a headmaster and a company director are so often cast in one conventional mould that they sound like blood brothers all making the same speech. But the fourth may be less formal and, while he may well be hated by the solicitor, headmaster and company director, he goes like a bomb, the audience receiving, at last, the entertainment they desired. So make sure that any speaker you ask is fully conversant with the traditions or needs of your function. Some are very versatile and can adapt their material to suit any occasion in brilliant style. But most of us are only horses for particular courses and it is unfair to put either speaker or audience out of their depth.

Speakers receiving in January an invitation to speak in October cannot always know their movements so far ahead. Ten months' notice is a bit wide, but nevertheless a committee is to be congratulated on making up its mind in plenty of time. Mostly speakers are invited for the following week! But a speaker, if given good notice, can accept on the proviso that, if he is not likely to be abroad on business, he will accept the date. Usually if he finds he cannot make it, he can give the organisers plenty of time to find a replacement. Or, as some can, find you a substitute themselves from their friends in the speaking world.

If in booking speakers, organisers used a professional agent, then he would find substitute speakers as part of the contract. However, it is doubtful if any speaker booked through an agency will let you down for any other reason save illness which is no one's fault. Yet it is odd that, if a speaker is sick and cannot turn up at the last minute, many organisers take it as a personal insult. The speaker's wife telephones her anxious regrets, but there is little sympathy either for her or the stricken speaker. The organiser, seeing his well-laid plans going to dust, almost accuses the bearer of the sad tidings of letting him down. Inevitably when the speaker writes an apologetic letter, it goes unanswered by the angry committee, who have dubbed him as 'unreliable'! 'Never again,' they say, 'he let us down!'

I suppose some speakers have feigned illness to get out of a date, but never a professional one. But committees engaging amateur speakers should always lay on standby speakers from within their own ranks. It stands to reason that, if another commitment comes up which considerably affects a speaker's career, then he must in all commonsense drop a totally fruitless speaking date, however pleasant the hospitality. Inviting the ordinary amateur speaker implies no contract, just goodwill, so the possibility of last minute cry-offs must be covered.

Briefing Speakers
Organisers of functions should brief all speakers or lecturers by letter. Phones lead to confusion and second-hand messages can easily be misunderstood. Many a dinner has been wrecked by the guest speaker being at the wrong venue ... he is at the George Hotel, Cleveleys, instead of the George, Cleethorpes ... who have never heard of him and are shut for the winter anyway! Which recalls the famous telegram G. K. Chesterton sent to his wife after setting out on a speaking date ... 'Am at Aylesbury – where should I be?'

Write personally to speakers, stating venue, time of reception, informal or black tie – or, if there is one, enclosing a printed ticket so that all the information is available. Add estimated time of closure and include any information to help him prepare his speech. The toast he is to propose, the objects of your society or products of your firm. Ask how he would like to be billed on the menu and how he wishes to be announced. The name of his overnight hotel or, if he is to receive private hospitality, the name and address of his host and hostess. Add all relevant phone numbers, including that of the venue itself, in case of delays through fog or accident.

And give him a deadline for his contribution. You cannot enforce a speaker to obey – but you can try! State in your letter: 'As this will be a very full evening with dance and cabaret to follow (or, if comprised of speeches only, mention the number of speakers) we shall only need to take up ten (or whatever) minutes of your time.'

Of course you will expect perhaps half an hour from your professional, your V.I.P. or star on a speakers-only bill. You are paying for that and, to ensure you get your return for the outlay, you must cut down on over-garrulous resident support-ing speakers. Even if your top-speaker is not charging a fee, he or she must still be given the courtesy of a good hearing. Certainly do not ask anyone to travel hundreds of miles just to make a ten minute speech. The short speeches must be the lot of your 'local' orators. I remember that splendidly amusing test cricketer and now television commentator, Jim Laker, being left with a mere eight minutes before an audience had to rush for the last train. He had come a long distance, was giving his services and yet the local monopolists egotistically ate up his more important time – and the audience was furious with a weak chairman who let them do so.

In such circumstances, if supporting speakers are liable to get hooked on their own verbosity or vie with your V.I.P. to outshine him, then confine the evening entirely to the chair-man's opening address and then let your main speaker have his head alone, just closing on a brief vote of thanks from the chair. If you are fortunate enough to have a good speaker who can hold an audience for a longish time, don't overload with others.

Chairmanship

Whether at a meeting or a public social function, the chairman is, in effect the captain of the ship – and, if he is either brash or nervous – he can sink it. A chairman is not necessarily your best speaker. Indeed if he is, his prowess will inevitably put the following speakers in the shade and a good start will be lost by later boredom. No chairman of the right mettle, even if he knows he has the ability, should allow this to happen anyway, but play himself down to the other's advantage.

A chairman should control the affair but not dominate it. We have all met the chairman who likes to be 'in-charge' and keeps bobbing up and down with remarks, interrupting the normal flow by continually forcing his presence on the room. A chairman should be firm, good-natured – but act *in support* of the speakers. Certainly he must not be too self-effacing or the toastmaster will have to take over if there is one in attendance. Nervous chairmen, possibly appointed by a roster system, are a danger to the entertainment value of an evening. If they waffle uncertainly about toilet intervals or keeping to time schedules, things can get out of hand. A chairman must plan his job carefully, timing every aspect, e.g. when the 'loyal' toast will be drank. Some, pandering to smokers, propose it too early – other delay it until coffee time. After the meat course is best but that should be decided during the committee planning time, so that everyone knows the drill and not as an after-thought on the night.

No chairman must show favouritism . . . inevitably he will have a guest either side of him and he must give them equal attention. I have seen some rather blatant one-upmanship when a chairman remains deep in conversation with the V.I.P. (or pretty woman) on his left and ignores the poor 'unknown' on his right – who has often been me !

A chairman's demeanour sets the tone of the function. He can be shrewd, witty – but never an out-and-out comedian. And if he is prone to make overlong speeches, then so will the other speakers, simply because they will follow his standard. A chairman must be utterly time-conscious throughout, even tactfully keeping the other speakers ever mindful of the clock.

No chairman should be wordy. Wrapping up ordinary state-ments in an oratorical manner is sheer vanity. A chairman must express himself concisely. His job is to impress the importance of the occasion, not himself. Elaborate perorations slow the evening up – or, if it is a business meeting, make the minutes very complicated to take down !

At meetings a chairman must ensure that the other speakers stick to the point and be prepared to guide them back if they stray. Decisions have to be made off-the-cuff, too, so you need a disciplined mind in that chair, capable of keeping order or enforcing it if heated argument looks like getting out of hand. And this must be done without obvious bias, not always easy when some minority fuss-pot keeps harping on some pet hobby horse.

Good chairmanship in management is vital today. Standards are changing. Companies as we know must expect less dedication and more self-centred interest from those they employ. It may sound a sad indictment of modern thinking, but it is cold, hard fact which has to be faced when chairing productivity and policy-making meetings. A wise chairman studies his meetings with the knowledge that everyone in the room is primarily interested in what is in it for him.

A chairman must never, at any function, forget to thank the organisers. He must acknowledge them formally at the end of the affair. He must always be sure of his facts. He must preside without being president; in effect, be retiring if all is going well and only dominant if some sudden rigid control is necessary. He is not a compère; too many confuse the jobs and make longish introductions, even sometimes to elaborating so much on the speaker to follow that the audience is put off before the poor devil rises. Some are gavel-happy and crash the table, setting the glasses ringing to get attention.

You can usually tell what sort of chairman you are in for by the way he uses a gavel. The timid tap the room cannot hear means you are in hesitant, unreliable hands; the pistol shots come from a dominant self-opinionated type who will lead from the front, anxious for personal limelight. But the crisp, disciplined staccato that does not make the top table guests put their hands over their ears will be the right man for the job.

The Job of Compère or Master-of-Ceremonies

By compère I use the term broadly. There are compères – and commères – beyond the variety performance and cabaret floor interpretation. The professional entertainer compère is a specialist, of course. I am one and try to relate my material, my jokes and comments to the event. I am not always right, even after thirty years of it, but I am rarely, nowadays, completely off the target. I have had experience of audiences and I know that if there is a successful comedian to round off the entertainment, I must not tell a funny story just before he comes on. My humour is reserved for linking the more serious acts, the singers, the instrumentalists, the speciality acts. But if a comedian or comedienne is on the bill – you announce them quickly and let *them* raise the laughs. Of course, in professional show business there is a lot of gamesmanship and bitchiness which can put a blot on an evening but, in the main, the professional knows his limitations far more than the amateur – and, of course, being paid to do the right thing means he suffers for it if he exceeds his engagement requirements.

But we can find ourselves compère or commère or master of ceremonies at many other occasions. Firms' dinners, informal company lunches and parties, even as host or hostess at our own parties, all need a form of master of ceremonies. If the occasion is sufficiently elaborate, of course, the company will hire a toastmaster, but many gatherings do not merit that expense. Also many functions need a man or woman officiating who KNOWS the business or event far more intimately than would an outside toastmaster whose duties are restricted to mere announcements. Business occasions often require an M.C. who is right hand man to the chairman of the occasion. Some events have unpredictable moments needing great experience in the project than any outside, professional or amateur, could possibly handle. Firms holding seminars and fortnight-long courses often use one of their bright employees as a major domo who can address classes, introduce lecturers and keep the schedule going with pace and verve. And he or she is also the 'information officer', to whom the humblest new student or the chairman himself can turn for guidance.

A good 'house-trained' compère or commère is a god-send to a firm. The duties are wider than Public Relations. He must not only be able to drive the train, but be able to stop and start it when authority commends. If he lets his own exuberant personality over-ride that duty, then the train will come off the rails. He has to remember that he is a producer of an already directed event. Any of you who have acted for a living or even amateurly will know there are some men and women who can produce a play quietly and effectively from the side-lines, while others are hell bent on giving a performance as producer themselves!

More and more firms today are using the 'master of ceremonies' technique in both business and social activities. He or she can take over the lesser duties of the chairman to leave him free to concentrate upon V.I.Ps and essential matters of policy on hand. A good compère or commère is not easy to find. You may well have to become a Baron Frankenstein and make yourself such a body, remembering that he did not aim to make a monster, it just turned out that way! If your firm needs such an official – a business friend of mine refers to 'his ring master' – you must train such a person. And it's easier to take a malleable type, the personality with an easy, relaxed manner, and discipline him or her into the more rigid duties of business occasions. They must be able to take instruction and yet possess a certain acting flair which can be adjusted to suit all occasions. It may be just a sideline from his or her normal duties in the firm, but, even if you employ an outside public relations company, have your own liaison officer within your own organisation.

The qualifications are a good administrative sense and an ability to stand up and speak in public. They should be called in on all briefings. Too often firms running a special event delegate only snippets of responsibility over a wide representation of employees, all of whom have to be co-ordinated often to the detriment of their normal work in the company. Let one man or woman handle the lot. If your M.C. has been involved from the start of the planning, he or she is fully briefed for the big day and in a position to control it from strength.

The office joker is not the man for the job, however fluent and entertaining his speeches are at the annual Christmas dinner. Any one liable to put his own personality first is wrong for the job. You need someone with a sense of occasion geared to the function, not to himself.

The hard-working but slightly neurotic employee who finds pessimistic hazards in everything he tackles for the firm is again not your man. He may be reliable to the n'th degree at his job, have a hundred per cent blameless record, but if he has fretted and fidgeted his way to that reliability he will not make a good organiser of big occasions. We all know the man who likes to be seen worrying about his job! A good leader keeps his anxieties to himself and only inflicts them upon others when he needs their positive expertise.

Beware, too, of the engaging adventurer who can 'con' you – and himself – into believing he is right for the job. I have met and had to deal with many who, by shooting some smooth line, have got the hot seat of responsibility by the sheer desire of achievement. Basically they are lazy people, prone to do business at bars rather than at desks. They seem efficient with their bonhomie but, in reality, are taking far too many chances with your money and time. They will delegate work like a spreading forest fire, using the phone assiduously. They don't mind talking a lot – they are phone drones – but find correspondence and going on personal calls rather like hard work. Often they resort to the phone, because they like a drink and don't want their breath noticed by superiors! Well-tailored, using good phraseology, they are the grasshopper-minded businessmen of today. But when emergencies arise they are found wanting – or cannot be found at all!

So your man or woman must be self-disciplined – and have true compassion. A sense of humour which can be controlled is also ideal. No one must expect a fierce overwhelming loyalty tantamount to bootlicking, but just a reasonable dedication. Too often directors expect an M.C. to act as a soulless lackey ... the real job is to take a lot of 'en route' chores off the chairman's hands – and be trusted to do so.

Frankly, I would interview a woman or two for commère duties. Ladies with office experience – I am married to one – have an additional sympathy not easily found in mere males. Their only handicap is that comparatively few women are called upon to make speeches or control big functions involving forms of personal public appearance. They are, of course, becoming more adept every day, but marriage, domestic life and raising families can always affect their business careers. But a good woman organiser or 'hostess' is a great boon to a firm. By her very sex she commands more than just tactful respect from juniors! Any seminar run with the woman's touch is inevitably a success – even to the flowers put in some otherwise very drab halls of instruction!

But, whether you select a man or woman for the job, you must be absolutely sure of their integrity. They are, of course, in the job for the money, but the prestige they obtain must be geared to the firm rather than from a sense of their own importance.

Open-Air Speaking

If you are called upon to address a meeting or perhaps compère an alfresco function, despite the use of a microphone, you must be absolutely concise in your approach. Outdoor audiences are far more likely to be diverted; there is much more to distract them than within four walls. At the slightest hint of dull speaking their eyes will wander around and absorb far more attractive objects.

Audiences do not knit together in the fresh air nearly so much as in numbered seats under a roof. There is that extra sense of freedom, so they rarely form into a set pattern or mood. Even a political speech out of doors needs to be pared down to its barest bones to make any real impact. There is also too much competition from people on the periphery of the gathering, passers-by who are determined not to be involved, but love to stand and stare, their ears closed to the words.

And if you are master of ceremonies or compère, only very short gags will be acceptable, one-liners preferably, before you get on with the vital announcements. If you are running a raffle, they want to hear the ticket number and colour clearly, *not* your jokes. Their minds are not on laughter, but on winning! Always remember that. I have heard many well-meaning compères at bazaars and fêtes, rambling on with mother-in-law and fish and chip stories getting no response whatsoever from a jostling throng who only want information as to where the beer tent is.

You will notice, when you introduce your star attraction or V.I.P. in the open air, that they, being experienced, will cut their address down to a couple of minutes at the outside. They know that such an audience will give even them only limited attention. There are, too, always children around, letting their lungs go, regardless of any formality on the rostrum ... so brevity is wise in the fresh air if you want to do your job correctly.

Always use a practical 'on' and 'off' switch on your microphone at alfresco functions. Otherwise muttered asides to the mayor can be heard all over the district. Leave a mike 'alive' and a passer-by stubbing his toe can use a four letter word which starts householders in the next county ringing the police.

And, if you are organising such a fête, check all amplification of sound. Nothing can be more annoying for a harmless citizen in his own home suddenly to hear music and disembodied voices shattering the peace of his Sabbath nap. When I commentated at the Oval during some of the first club Sunday competition games, we had many an irate phone call; the local residents had put up with it all the week, now suddenly their day of rest was ruined. So we kept all announcements to a minimum. It was only fair.

Check, then, with local police and have your engineers arrange your amplifiers to create the least possible nuisance to surrounding homes.

EXERCISE *Use as practice for an instructional 'talk', items from 'Chairmanship' onwards. Take each one as a separate short speech to students or employees. Rehearse them first and, if you can, put them on tape, just to hear if you sound 'in authority'. You can edit 'me' out if you like but it does not matter much at this stage. But be yourself – don't pretend you are 'me'!*

CHAPTER TEN

Appearing on Television and Radio

Time was when to have been heard on the radio or seen on the 'telly', meant everlasting fame in your street. But not any more. Today more and more people from wider fields are called upon to voice their opinions over the air. You are no longer special now if your face and voice appears in receivers. However it remains a severe test of personality just the same.

The microphone picks up every syllable, every falter, every 'um' and 'er'. And the need for clear thinking and a good vocabulary is vital if you are not to sound indecisive or lame.

Television
You may find yourself as part of the general public during some newsworthy situation, such as a train strike, when you are asked at random for your views. An interviewer sticks a microphone in front of you and says: 'How do you feel about it?'

You have to think really quickly, be mentally alert to give a respectable answer worthy of yourself. You have no time for preamble, you have to make a definite statement . . . You either agree with the strike or you don't . . . You must say something concrete . . . If you don't, you will look in vain for your face to come up when the pre-filmed interviews are shown on the screen. They will have cut it out because you waffled, couldn't collect yourself, couldn't go beyond saying the strike was a good or bad thing. And if you have told friends 'I'm on the telly tonight' you can look pretty stupid if you are omitted.

It is possession of a working vocabulary and precision of thinking that makes some people good before cameras and others woefully weak. Dialects don't matter – it is clarity, both orally and mentally, which counts.

Going a step further, you might well be interviewed in a studio in connection with your job, hobby or political grievance. Mostly the interviewer will be opposite you and put the questions. This is comparatively easy if you don't fidget in front of the camera. But it can happen with these last-minute interviews that you may be in one studio with a cameraman and an interviewer, in voice only, asks you the questions from some hundred miles away. This system, while necessary for nine-day wonder topics, is not easy for you if you are going out 'live', that is, not being pre-filmed but being seen by the viewing public at that very moment. Nothing can be edited out – your faults will be shown if you make any.

Also the time factor will be taken into account. You have to be quick. The interviewer often ends a short discussion with: 'Can you tell me in the 15 seconds remaining, briefly what you think should be done . . .' That is a hell on earth for anyone, however experienced, rather like that always questionable court-room tactic used by counsel of 'Answer "yes" or "no",' to a question which obviously needs some qualification for answering either way. But programmes are timed to the second, especially on ITV where 'commercials' have to appear as per contract, so there is no place for the waffler.

Beware, too, that you are never guilty of 'catching the tone' of the interviewer. This is often a hazard with beginners, even in after-dinner or business speeches. A nervous young speaker follows a mature orator – and sounds just like an imitation of him! He has subconsciously caught his tone, taking an instinctive refuge in the fact that, if the previous speaker's 'sound' pleased the audience, then he must repeat it. This is the copyist mind at work . . . on the look-out for short-cuts rather than develop his own personality. And on TV 'tone-catching' is even more apparent for the interviewer comes back into the dialogue all the time so the imitation is even more transparent.

This often occurs when the subject repeats the interviewer's question . . . 'You ask me, have I ever been to Berlin . . . well . . .' In that very repetition he can adopt the interviewer's tone, make the question sound exactly the same in timbre, enunciation and, if the question has been asked in a regional dialect, faithfully reproduce that as well! So, to avoid this fault, do not repeat the question. It wastes valuable time anyway. No, pause and think before you reply. You cannot consider your answer with a clear mind if you are still repeating his words. So – pause – then come straight out with your reply . . . 'I was in Berlin in 1973 . . .'

While, at present, appearing on television might seem remote, still study the technique on your own screen at home. Watch all points. Remember that more and more firms are training their employees to face cameras, for television has wider connotations in the business world than just entertaining the populace. 'Talks' can be sent abroad on film to be projected to associated companies, whole meetings can be held on closed circuit television without any of the participants leaving their desks. So attune your mind to it, polish up the vocabulary and diction – and think as finely as a razor's edge. For if you don't, someone else will.

Radio
With 'local' radio stations now holding a very defiant grip, despite television, on many areas in Britain, you will almost certainly be asked to appear if you have a reputation in your home town as a public speaker. The interview is always straightforward – but giving a talk is not so simple as it sounds. If you have been used to audiences and the atmospheric hum they generate, you can find the cold silence of a sound-proofed studio somewhat nerve wracking. Speaking as a disc jockey in short bursts is comparatively simple if you have scripted the programme properly and don't try and do it 'off-the-cuff' as so many do today – with some rather feeble results. But giving a sustained talk, if it is going out 'live', is a very delicate operation. It is far better to have it put on tape so that you have the additional assurance that any fluffs you make can be edited out.

The system when 'taping' a talk is that if you should fluff, mispronounce or cough into a word, you pause five seconds and go back to the beginning of that paragraph or sentence. Never try and take up again just the 'fluff' because it will rarely match the tone-quality of the previous words. Having lost the rhythm of the sentence, you cannot pick it up midstream. You return to the last full stop or, better, the beginning of the paragraph and start that section again. The five second gap allows the editor space to get his scissors in to make the cut and to overlap and rejoin the tape again.

Few talks need to go out 'live' today, unless they are last-minute assignments, and then the speakers are usually people of already great experience. Speaking from a script does cancel out the 'ums' and 'ers', so keep your wits about you. And try not to start each sentence with 'Well, er . . .'

Listen to radio talks and watch television for techniques as much as you can. Even if the subject may not be your cup of tea, watch the more educational programmes such as Open University, when publicly-unknown experts discuss their projects. You will hear new words and see the repose of the speakers. Put yourself in their shoes and always remember that a camera is in front of them, not a 'live' audience. Yet millions are viewing . . . so, if you can make a successful impact, you will certainly spread your gospel, with far-reaching results!

A lesser, but useful hint concerns participation in the radio or TV 'Phone-in' type of programme. Listeners and viewers are requested to telephone before or during programmes, giving their questions to a panel of experts. Brevity is essential, time is the overriding factor, yet some members of the public still do NOT write out their queries first – they get on the line, waste valuable seconds by over-elaborate courtesies, or call the interviewer, whom they have never met, by his christian name! – and then blunder out their viewpoint with all the 'ums', 'ers' and 'didn't I's'. Write down your question first, prune it to the bare sense – and *read* it out. That not only ensures a clear answer without a lot of qualifying queries from the experts, but allows more participants to take part in the time available.

I notice this tendency to get on the wire quite unprepared often on my local radio station. They have an extremely good 'exchange and mart' type of programme, when listeners offer articles for sale or exchange over the air, phoning in during the programme to state their offerings and name and address. Many a dear housewife seems to get on just for a chat! If she has some old 78 records to dispose of, she doesn't know how many or what titles they are – so she has to leave the phone to check!

It is most frustrating for the most efficient young master of ceremonies, who is constantly up against the clock.

So write all the details down for any phone-in programme – and then you will sound cool and efficient – for, after all, you *are* speaking in public – to millions!

EXERCISE : *Use this whole chapter as an instructional talk. Edit it where you think you might use terms more typical of yourself than me if you like but rehearse it first thoroughly. Then try it out just to get the 'feel' of imparting information in a practical way without emotive over-tones.*

CHAPTER ELEVEN

The Public Speaker who will be you

With a billion species of personalities inhabiting the world, no really promising public speaker can ever be lead entirely by the hand. Each individual has his or her own creative sense. So they may baulk at certain safety measures I advocate, possibly contradict certain facets which have proved successful in my own case. That I fully understand for I have broken many rules too simply because I would not have been true to myself if I had slavishly obeyed them to the letter. But the solid foundation on which they are founded has allowed me to adjust. If you ever heard me speak I would beseech you to do as I say rather than as I do!

What I have attempted in this book is to show you the surest way to absorb experience. Like an actor playing a part, he needs to know the rudiments of back-stage workings. I cannot visualise you as a person, naturally, but I can help prevent you wandering off on uncharted paths in a particularly exposed world. Mistakes in public speaking are sometimes hard to live down and are almost always made by the inexperience of 'layman technique', seeing the speaking business only from the front rather than know its backroom workings.

Once you have put in a few consistent speaking months, facing audiences, some suggestions I have made in these pages you may well discard as not being quite 'you'. So be it. But if you are a real beginner then I hope I have helped to get you started and have prevented you from suffering too much disillusionment through early failure. But once that testing time is over, then I do expect you to go a-roving in your own personalised way.

As I say goodbye all I ask is that you think of your audiences and give them what they want – which may not necessarily be what you think they want. And you will know from gathering experience just how successful you are at pinpointing audiences' tastes. If they invite you back again, you are a good speaker; if not then you will have to change your tune in that particular sphere. But they are not, of course, the criterion of all audiences so you must be patient and study the job from all angles. Then there will come a time when you give them *all* what they want.

Your aim must be sincerity. Truth is both power – and beauty.

One last thought. If you can bring up your children to be unafraid to face audiences, to look people in the eye and argue without intolerance, you will be doing the world – and them – a service. The future is in their hands. Equip them to speak well by giving them confidence, love and, above all, your enthusiasm.